# UNSTOPPABLE

KERRYN GAMBLE

First published by Busybird Publishing 2016

Copyright © 2016 Kerryn Gamble

ISBN

Print ISBN: 978-0-9945839-9-4

Ebook ISBN: 978-0-9946156-0-2

Kerryn Gamble has asserted her right under the Copyright, Designs and Patents Act 1988 to be identified as the author of this work. The information in this book is based on the author's experiences and opinions. The publisher specifically disclaims responsibility for any adverse consequences, which may result from use of the information contained herein. Permission to use information has been sought by the author. Any breaches will be rectified in further editions of the book.

All rights reserved. No part of this publication may be reproduced, stored in or introduced into a retrieval system, or transmitted in any form, or by any means (electronic, mechanical, photocopying, recording or otherwise) without the prior written permission of the author. Any person who does any unauthorised act in relation to this publication may be liable to criminal prosecution and civil claims for damages. Enquiries should be made through the publisher.

Cover image: Zahrina Robertson

Cover design: Busybird Publishing

Layout and typesetting: Busybird Publishing

Editor: Melissa Cleeman

Busybird Publishing
PO Box 855
Eltham Victoria
Australia 3095

www.busybird.com.au

# Testimonials

Kerryn has given me clarity of purpose, confidence to inspire and focussed results in business.

– *Ros Weadman, Director,* Melbourne PR & Marketing

Kerryn took me from a place of lacking attention, focus and drive, to a place of empowerment and motivation to succeed in my current goals.

– *Jenny Clencie, Director,* Level 10 With Jen

Interesting and useful for work and relationships. I feel I'm better able to understand and connect with my clients.

– *Judy Bond, Senior Property Manager,* Harcourts

What an inspirational person! Kerryn's helped me hone in and get crystal clear on the value I bring to my audience and amplify this in business.

– *Anna Perdriau, Owner,* Destination Excellence

Not only did I clear away blockages, I also became very clear as to what my purpose was in my business.

*— Caroline Seipp, Owner,* Direct Connection

Kerryn comes at personal development and leadership from a completely different perspective. It's like she has opened up my head and put new ideas in there! Not just ideas, but practical measures to develop my leadership style.

*— Philip Bendeich, Director,* SCAX Consulting

Thanks to Kerryn, I learned more about myself and really honed in on what my platform is.

*— Yakira, Freelance Writer*

I have achieved amazing breakthroughs in both my personal life and my business growth. I have addressed some deep seated issues from the past that had held me back from achieving all I am capable of. I now have more power, freedom and peace of mind to move forward with my own personal journey.

*— Julieanne Beck,* New'Be'Leaf Coaching

Kerryn provided just the support I needed to help me find much needed clarity in my present situation and the confidence and commitment to move forward.

– *Debbie Brownhill*

Kerryn, you managed to have me physically implement actions that I have been wanting to attack for some time now. I have the ability to keep the momentum going and more of a 'can do' attitude. Instead of just thinking about all the things I would like to do, I am now armed with the ability to turn my thoughts into actions.

– *Pam White*

To my surprise, I am amazed how much I have learned about myself and the knowledge I have gained to handle certain situations.

– *Elvira Saric*

# Dedication

*For women who dare and women who do
– together we make the world a better place.*

# Contents

| | |
|---|---|
| Introduction | 1 |
| **PART 1 - PURPOSE** | 7 |
| Confidence Zone | 9 |
| Recalibration | 27 |
| Mini Me | 37 |
| Multiple Dimensions | 51 |
| **PART 2 - POWER** | 65 |
| Compelling Communication | 67 |
| Unspoken Edge | 77 |
| CongruentCurrency | 87 |
| Re-Wire | 99 |
| **PART 3 - PROSPERITY** | 111 |
| New You | 113 |
| Authentic Influence | 121 |
| Action Traction | 133 |
| Rapid Results | 143 |
| Afterword | 149 |
| Acknowledgements | 151 |
| About the Author | 152 |
| Working With Kerryn | 154 |
| Confidence Magnifier Guide | 157 |
| Kerryn as a Speaker | 159 |
| Woman of Worth Program | 162 |
| Resources – Values Elicitation Activity | 166 |
| Resources | 173 |

# Introduction

Around the bend into the final straight, glimpsing the finish line, I gave it everything. With heart pounding, lungs on fire and mouth gasping for air, I knew I had to find a way to keep going – to stay focussed on the finish and distract from the pain of the moment. I felt on the verge of passing out and vomiting and spontaneous combustion felt completely possible. I desperately wanted to find a way to maintain the intensity and not be consumed by it. Mentally, I went to a different place, my mind switched to an unfamiliar channel, creating an outer body experience. Momentarily, my awareness shifted from the physical to that of a curious observer. I became aware of my cheeks flapping in a way they never had and the taste of blood in my mouth. I was watching myself run the race of my life. I had separated the mental from the physical. Then the 400m sprint was over.

With legs shaking and pulse hammering, I felt a mix of familiar and unfamiliar sensations: relief and realisation. I had never pushed myself like this before. It didn't feel good, I didn't like it and yet, this became a defining moment; an important lesson and a clue leading to future accomplishments.

This sprint event was the last race on the last day of the athletics season. It was also my last chance to earn enough points achieve my *red ribbon*, a ribbon reflecting a level of performance across all track and field categories according to set benchmarks. It was something I coveted.

I was eight-years-old and this was the first time I had really backed myself. In comparison to others in my age category, my athletic ability and results hovered around the average range. My early experiences had resulted in disqualification for (successful) dive rolls over the high jump bar and for a discus throw hitting a volunteer standing behind me! To my surprise in an 800m walk, I took off and came close to lapping a fellow competitor. My first thought was that I must be doing something wrong, so I slowed down to wait for others to catch up, feeling more comfortable being among the group, than being alone out in front.

The parallels between sporting foibles and life are strikingly similar: finding yourself discounted or disqualified when you don't know (or follow) the rules, having a go at something new and not doing well, being prepared, persevering to get the results you want, and feeling alone out front.

The themes in my journey are experienced by many women and rather than bury them, I want to share them. What I've discovered through ongoing personal development, much soul searching and coach training is that results for our personal and professional lives begin from within.

The turning point in my life came when I shifted from having a go, to committing wholeheartedly. What's been instrumental along the way is acknowledging the discomfort of doing something unfamiliar, but not using this as a reason to avoid or discontinue action. I have used a results-focussed mindset for outcomes ranging from curing myself of a needle phobia, winning a gold medal in a national aerobics competition and even writing this book. It's the same results-focused mindset I use when working with clients.

Shifts in mindset are powerful. Removing limiting beliefs and replacing them with more empowering ones is life changing. I have seen clients come to life through developing clarity of purpose, feeling more confident and taking action on dream projects. Beyond personal growth, clients experience professional growth in a range of ways – establishing business partnerships, attracting new clients, boosting brand visibility and tripling their turnover.

I believe women are the future of business and drivers of the economy. In a Sydney Morning Herald article, *MasterCard says Australian retail sales 'worrisome'*, Sarah Quinlan, MasterCard's Senior Vice President of marketing insights, suggests women make three-quarters of all retail transactions in Australia. We have valuable instincts and insights when it comes to marketing, sales and purchase decisions. If we make purchase decisions based on what we want and/or need, then who better to be closely involved with design, production, marketing, sales and innovation than women? After all, women understand women – we know how we think, what we value, what we really need and why we're more likely to purchase Product A over Product B.

Despite this, we also seem to have a generation of super-achieving women with the highest levels of anxiety and depression in history. We're educated and liberated, but not yet empowered. The need to be liked, fear of rejection and fear of not being good enough are crippling the personal and professional lives of many women. It's unnecessary and it's time to change *now*.

There's a confidence gap stretching across professions, income levels and generations. The confidence gap exists even where you may not expect to find it – among highly successful women. At the heart of this is our self-worth. Dictionary.com defines self-worth as, 'the sense of one's own value or worth as a person'. The great news is, how we feel about ourselves is up to us. Self-worth is like a personal bank account; we have the ability to choose an account with compounding interest or one with high fees. We choose our account set up and the frequency of deposits. The greater our self-worth investment, the less impact unexpected fees or withdrawals have. A commitment to consistent regular deposits is a wise investment approach, making self-worth the ultimate investment for all women.

When self-worth is fuelled externally through praise and positive feedback, we are at risk of becoming dependent on our environment to feel okay about ourselves, and in the face of criticism (real or perceived), we may become easily defensive or withdrawn. Praise, positive feedback and acknowledgment make us feel great – unless we believe we don't deserve it! We're wired to want to contribute, grow and feel important at times. Is your relationship with praise one of dependence or one of delight? Do you feel you *need* praise and approval from others or is this an unexpected source of feeling good? When we're held captive by our perception of who we need to be, to feel accepted or good enough, our sense of personal worth becomes skewed. I call this *distorted-worth syndrome.*

So how does perfectionism fit into this? There's a fine line between being a high achiever and a perfectionist. Men and women who are prone to self-doubt, chase perfectionism to mask their low self-worth. A high achiever wants to be better for their own personal growth and satisfaction, whilst a perfectionist wants to be better to satisfy others. Wanting to be better to satisfy *ourselves*, compared to satisfying *others* is a subtle yet important distinction.

I used to be a perfectionist. Thinking back, I can recall declaring this with a tinge of pride in my voice. My old view of perfectionism was that it meant I had high standards. Since then, I've learned that perfectionism means you have *no* standards. Think about it: a perfectionist does everything to one perfect standard, without awareness of context or ability to adapt their efforts accordingly. A perfectionist has only one way of approaching a task. The context of your goal determines your approach. For example, if you're writing a book and you want it to be a New York Times Best Seller, your work will need to be of a very high standard. Compare this to writing a how-to book; the grammar and sentence structure doesn't need to be the same calibre for the book to be effective and successful.

What I've experienced and continue to see with clients is smart, talented women not communicating the value they bring to what they do. That value being their *personal currency*. My vision is a world where women communicate their worth with conviction. My mission of closing the confidence and achievement gap is driven by being shy during childhood, feeling invisible and believing my opinions and ideas were not as valuable as my highly-intelligent sibling. The turning point in my life was not speaking up when I needed to, which almost cost me my life.

I wrote this book to assist women in connecting with their unique talents, building personal currency and move beyond their perceived fear of not being enough. I want readers to tap into their zone of confidence for greater personal power and prosperity.

This book is written in three parts: Part One relates to the inner work that's needed to get clear on what matters and being okay to be you. Part Two is about leveraging your personal currency to set yourself apart and stand out, and Part Three focuses on moving beyond your comfort zone for greater prosperity. Each chapter explores these elements in more depth and follows with self-discovery through reflection activities and resources.

If you're an employee, this book will provide the stepping stones to a more empowered you in the workplace and help you avoid self-sabotaging habits common among women. If you're in business or thinking of starting your own business, this book will help you discover specific tactics to communicate with more credibility, congruence and influence to build and grow a successful business. When you follow the suggested steps at the end of each chapter, you will now notice a shift in how you feel about your personal currency.

If you've had enough of being who you think you should be and you're ready to live life from a place of worthiness, then congratulations on taking the first step towards becoming your UNSTOPPABLE self!

# PART ONE

# PURPOSE

# 1
# Confidence Zone

*Don't ask what the world needs. Ask what makes you come alive and go do it. Because what the world needs is people who have come alive.*

~ Howard Thurman

Confidence is less about what you've been born with and more about what you make of yourself. Confidence separates those who imagine from those who do. There are plenty of people with great ideas who don't take that next step to bring their ideas to life. For a while, I was one of those people.

Shortly before the birth of my second child, I accepted a redundancy package. It was perfect timing – I could stay at home with my two under two and return to work on my terms when I was ready. There I was, living the dream of no pressures to have to work, being at home with my gorgeous baby and toddler. Yet, I was becoming increasingly unhappy. After re-surfacing from months of very little sleep, I could no longer ignore the internal restlessness. The opportunity I had been looking forward to, was feeling increasingly like a prison sentence.

I felt guilty – really guilty! I knew of friends and colleagues who were not able to have children or subsequent pregnancies, and after my own experience of several miscarriages, I was grateful to have safely carried and delivered my two children. Yet, the internal feelings continued to grow and I became increasingly unhappy. I thought this was going to be a fulfilling experience – and it was. It was a mixture of rewarding moments that made my heart sing, along with mind-numbing boredom and isolation.

As weeks became months and months turned into years, the flame that existed within became smaller and smaller and I knew I needed to do something. I didn't want to take on another project management role, similar to what I'd been doing previously. Instead, I wanted to make a difference with what I was doing and feel deeply connected to my work. I didn't know specifically what that career looked like or what it might be. The tipping point came when the risk of losing myself felt more dangerous than the risk of having a go at something. So I made the first move to rediscover who I was and how I might make a difference.

The most challenging part of taking action was taking the first step, because I didn't specifically know what I wanted. I started to research, reached out to my network, began reading personal development books and made contact with organisations who offered courses that were of interest. Once I had some momentum, it became a lot easier to take the next step. I began to feel happier, I was pro-actively doing something to change my current situation. A large part of my journey and the foundation for the work I do, has been developing greater self-awareness.

During the time at home with my baby and toddler, I felt I didn't know who I was any more – I felt disconnected from doing meaningful work. Yet, I shared a desire to be present for my children during their early years, based on my belief that this was important and meaningful. As my self-awareness grew, so did my self-confidence. I learned through greater self-awareness comes greater self-confidence in who we are, what our personal currency is and how we make a difference. I call this our confidence zone. When you decide to move forward and take the first step towards what really matters to you, you develop your confidence zone.

Author, Katy Kay, claims success correlates more closely with confidence than it does with competence in her book, *The Confidence Code*. As technology evolves, existing career roles become obsolete and new ones are created. This places even more importance on skills transferability, as well as awareness of our unique talents and belief in our capabilities.

Confidence is like a magnifier of our talents and strengths, and with this comes a certain energy. You may have experienced this firsthand when you've been out and met someone with an energy that created a lasting impression. You may not know specifically what it was, but you remember their presence and how it felt to be around them.

Confidence is not related to extroversion. Whilst an extrovert might be more obvious in a room, confidence is equally attainable for both introverts and extroverts. How do you know if you're an introvert or extrovert? I believe the definition revolves around energy balance and the answer to this question: when you're feeling low in energy, what is the most effective way for you to recharge? Is it chilling out by yourself (reading, listening to music, going for a walk, meditating, etc.), or is it by picking up the phone and getting a group of friends together? A true introvert will need time out by themselves to recharge. Their batteries are on the inside. Whereas a true extrovert needs to be surrounded by people, movement and sound to recharge. An extrovert has batteries on the outside.

I believe we are not one or the other. I believe introversion and extroversion exist along a continuum. Two extroverts or introverts can show different levels of extroversion or introversion. With an appreciation for energy exchange and your own preferences, you're in a position to recognise when you need time away versus time with others. It also means if someone declines your invitation and tells you they need some timeout, it's not a personal rejection. They're communicating what they need to maintain their energy and function at their best.

*Self-confidence is that energy.* Self-confidence is being okay within yourself, so that you can be truly present for others. Being present is more than just turning up. It's about taking an interest in what others are saying and what's happening around you. If you're having a judgemental conversation in your head (perhaps about what you just said), then you have less head space available to focus on those around you.

I believe self-confidence is essential for creating sustainable, rewarding personal and professional outcomes. Self-confidence creates opportunities to contribute examples of female leadership within your business, your organisation, your community and your family.

> *When nothing is sure, everything is possible.*
> ~ Margaret Drabble

I remember cold calling early on in my business. I was running my first public workshop called, 'Unlock Your Team's Potential'. I'd left it too late to market the event, so I decided to door knock all relevant local businesses as a way to drum up interest and have people register. Previously, the idea of cold calling was stressful and something I would have avoided at all costs. This time my mindset was different. I had just completed NLP Training (Neuro-Linguistic Programming) and was feeling confident, calm and certain.

For three days, I walked into all related businesses within a short radius of where the workshop was being held. I asked to speak with the Director or Team Manager and proceeded to ask him/her about their team and the communication among the staff. I positioned the workshop as a great step to improving team dynamics and team communication within their business, as well as a step forward to improving the relationships with their suppliers.

After all this, only eight people attended the workshop, with five of those being friends or colleagues of mine! It may not have been a successful marketing campaign, but it was a successful activity. Through the process of taking action and cold calling door-to-door, I met a business director who was impressed with my attitude and energy, and invited me on the spot to train his team. This lead to a great working relationship with a major real estate group, spanning three years.

A study published in the Journal of Occupational and Organisational Psychology, showed women who displayed both male and female traits of confidence are promoted more than men displaying stereotyped masculine traits, or women displaying stereotyped female confidence traits. This suggests women who adapt their behavioural style are perceived as more competent and more suited to leadership roles.

Organisations are recognising this and seeking ways to increase women among their management and leadership teams. Interestingly, the approach by some women to seek more senior roles is to discount themselves before the selection process has begun. A Hewlett Packard study aimed at getting more women into management, showed women will only apply for a position if they meet 100% of the job requirements. In comparison, men were comfortable to apply after meeting 60% of the job requirements listed. This suggests women feel confident to take the next steps when they feel confident or 'perfectly qualified' according others' criteria, versus a belief in their ability to grow and learn on the job.

There's a range of estimates for how much genetics contribute to our innate confidence based on studies comparing fraternal with paternal twins. Katy Kay shares these findings in *The Confidence Code* and suggests genetics may contribute up to 50% of the innate confidence we're born with. According to these statistics, we can equally influence our genetic predisposition and self-confidence – that's great news if you feel your confidence could do with a boost!

What does a lack of self-confidence mean for women in business? Linda Babcock, author of *Nice Girls Don't Ask,* found in studies with business school students, that men initiate salary negations four times more than women. And when women do initiate, they ask for 30% less. Why do women ask for less? Deep down we still seem to believe we are worth 20% to 30% less than men!

Building on this, Professor Marilyn Davidson, co-author of *Women in Management*, surveys her business school students about what they *expect* to earn and what they *deserve* to earn five years after graduation. On average, the men's expectations were greater than women's, by around 20%. Professor Davidson claims lower expectations by women, stems from their lack of confidence.

Business is taking the contribution women make to the bottom line seriously. In *Womenomics*, authors Claire Shipman and Katy Kay describe how the Norwegian Government has become so convinced about the value of women in business, they introduced board quotas of 40% in 2003. From 2006 it became compulsory for all companies in Norway to have 40% or more women on their company boards. An article published in *The Conversation*, reviewed the status of this initiative ten years after its introduction. The article explains that companies were more financially successful, showed greater innovation and board effectiveness ten years after this quota was introduced, compared to companies with less than 40% of women on their board.

The evidence is overwhelming. Independent research firm, Catalyst, published an article titled, *Companies With More Women Board Directors Experience Higher Financial Performance, According to Latest Catalyst Bottom Line Report*. In this article, former Catalyst president, Ilene Lang, comments on the strong correlation between corporate performance across three important metrics and gender diversity. The bottom line is, in organisations where gender diversity is well managed, financial measures excel. The *2007 Catalyst Bottom Line Report* showed, Fortune 5000 companies with the highest representation of female board directors attained higher financial performance on average, than those with the lowest representation of women board directors.

Having women on boards is important because this is where opinions are sought and decisions affecting the broader community are made. We talk about the glass ceiling as an external barrier yet I believe, and what I continue to see with clients, is that women hold themselves back with their thinking, their language and their physicality.

A distinction I want to make is between confidence and self-confidence: I believe there's a difference, and a definition I have found useful and embrace is by Dr Julian Short, an Australian psychiatrist. Dr Short describes *confidence* as, 'knowing you can do something', and *self-confidence* as, 'knowing you're fine if you can't'. Knowing you can do something provides an inner certainty. Being fine if you can't do something, is an empowering mindset, freeing us to take action with an attitude of acceptance and openness to have a go without being paralysed by doubt.

What happens when we're under-confident? Essentially, under-confidence equals inaction. Under-confidence means we hesitate because we're unsure. We hold ourselves back, we feel the need to do more research, to ask for more opinions, and get more advice. We come up with elegant justifications to explain why we can't or why now is not the right time to do something. There is rarely a right time! Remember, confidence is situational. We feel a whole lot more confident in areas where we have experience. So it's natural not to feel confident when we're attempting to do something new.

The term 'confidence' is often used interchangeably with 'self-confidence'. I believe a marker of self-confidence is taking action, trying new things and having a go. It's natural to want to be seen in a positive way. The ability to be wrong, make a mistake and *be okay* with making a mistake, requires letting go of what others might think. This doesn't mean you won't be disappointed. I believe there are three dimensions to self-confidence: the *thinking*, the *language* and the *movement* – what we believe, what we say and what we do.

I had a client who proclaimed, 'I'm just not a confident person!' Her statement was made with such conviction, she sounded completely confident about her lack of confidence!

## 3 DIMENSIONS OF SELF CONFIDENCE

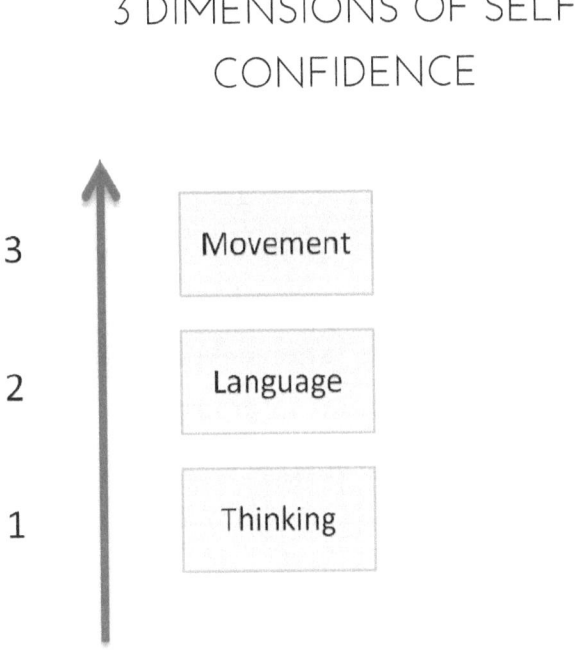

How do you build more self-confidence? One way is to believe you have value to contribute and the other is taking action. Embracing challenge builds confidence. Confidence comes from doing, from taking a step outside of your comfort zone, be it a few millimetres or a few miles. In those moments of feeling stretched or unsure about having a go, we're growing and compounding our personal value. I appreciate it's easy to say and more difficult to do when we're experiencing emotions such as fear.

Historically, fear was a survival mechanism, helping to keep us safe from danger (such as hungry animals). We needed to be aware of anything threatening or unusual to maximise our chance of survival. The physical feeling we associate with fear is created by the release of stress hormones. Interestingly, our brain releases stress hormones, regardless of whether the threat is real or imagined. Our body responds to these stress hormones by increasing our heart rate and breathing. When we experience fear, we have one of three responses: fight, flight or freeze. With low self-confidence, the flight and freeze reflexes are more common.

In her book, *Playing Big*, Tara Mohr describes two different types of fear: one is keeping us safe from possible failure and the other is keeping us safe from the other extreme – possible *fabulousness*. In the first instance, our ego wants to protect us physically and emotionally. In the second instance, our ego is protecting us from purposeful potential – the possibility of doing something way beyond what we've ever done before. This fear relates to vulnerability of what others may think and feeling exposed. This includes sharing our voice, our messages, our thoughts, our talents and our creativity – anything that reveals the real us.

In the context of self-confidence, these two types of fear both lead to a similar outcome, which is inaction. Inaction keeps us safe, prevents us from taking chances and in turn, hinders us from pursuing our dreams if we let it.

Fear of the unknown journey ahead can feel overwhelming at times, giving us a sense that we're not ready or need to be better equipped to take on something new. Self-confidence is a decision rather than a *feeling*. Yet, for some women, their decision to act is based on *feeling*. So, when something doesn't feel right, it's perceived as intuition steering them away from a bad choice rather than the discomfort of doing something unfamiliar.

Growing up, I believed I was average. I remember attending appointments with my brother, who was (according to assessment tools used at the time), measuring off the charts intelligence. One day, I decided to ask if I could do one of these tests to see if I was special like him. I completed one of the tests and with anticipation, awaited my results. I was told I was *just average.* They were the words I recall being used – I'll never know whether that's what was said or my interpretation of what was said.

Being a young girl, I took this to mean that my ideas, opinions or input were not particularly valuable. This impacted how I thought about myself, what I thought I was capable of and how I made decisions. This had a flow-on effect in all areas of my life: hobbies and extracurricular activities, school subjects, university courses, career choices and even choices of relationship partners! I made choices that *felt* comfortable and decisions that reaffirmed feeling average. Now, I see challenges as opportunity for growth and the pathway to next level results and essential for ongoing personal development.

Self-confidence plays a significant role in how we approach and make decisions. If you have a tendency to put off decisions that feel uncomfortable, here's a process to guide your thinking:

- **Why do you believe this feeling is coming up now?**
- **What's the purpose of the opportunity/decision?**
- **How is this opportunity/decision connected to what you care about?**
- **How is this moving you towards a desired outcome?**
- **Who else does this effect or impact?**

Discomfort during decision making is sometimes a values clash or a signal that you're stretching your comfort zone and testing your beliefs about your self-worth. An example of a values clash is deciding whether to accept a promotion that keeps you away from your family and home for longer periods. Whilst the promotion might move you towards a professional outcome you desire, it's conflicting with your personal core value of family time. Alternatively, if the promotion is a step up and your self-confidence is low, then you won't *feel* ready, and your discomfort at accepting the offer is connected to not *feeling* certain in your ability to do the job. Next time you feel discomfort when making a decision, ask yourself: is the feeling related to a values clash or is it keeping me safe from personal growth and feeling vulnerable about the future?

Have you or someone you know ever said, 'I'm just not a confident person'? I've heard many women say this over the years. I believe confidence has been unfairly perceived as a domineering attribute, used for bragging about talents and successes.

Historically, a woman displaying assertive and ambitious behaviour, was not necessarily viewed as self-confident. Instead, she was sometimes referred to using terms such as dominating, domineering, ballsy or a real bitch. In a 2014 article published by Chartered Management Institute, Moya Greene, Chief Executive of the UK's Royal Mail (one of only five women globally in a FTSE 100 CE post), claims women with leadership ambitions are constantly thwarted by negativity.

Traditionally, confidence was perceived as a masculine quality. A quality deemed desirable by men, particularly those in leadership or management roles. Women who demonstrate similar confidence behaviours to men, can be perceived unfavourably. In Harvard Business Review article, *For Women Leaders, Likability and success Hardly Go Hand-in-Hand*, Marianne Cooper, reports a backlash against powerful women, with descriptions such as 'ball-breaker' being used to describe them. For these reasons, women are not keen to put themselves in situations where they could be perceived as unfeminine or undesirable. For many women, the need to be liked is a strong driving force.

As you grow and evolve you may experience the challenge of shifting outdated beliefs around women communicating with confidence. There may be push back, sometimes by those closest to you. Many women I've worked with and spoken to have said, 'I want to be confident in a feminine way. I don't want to be ballsy and I don't want to be thought of as a bitch. I want to be able to show my emotions without judgement of being weak or overly emotional'. Women value friendships and are more likely to be driven by connection. The untrue belief that you can't demonstrate confidence and still be connected with your emotional side, creates a false stress for some women.

Traditionally, women have held roles of care-givers, homemakers and nurturers. I believe at the core of these roles is a vision for a happy healthy future, an awareness of key areas that contribute to this, a desire to make things happen and an ability to support and include others. These are valuable and desirable skills for any environment and particularly relevant to workplaces today.

Women in leadership bring inclusiveness to the workplace. Organisations are now experiencing the most disengaged workforce ever. According to the Deloitte University Press report, *Global Human Capital Trends 2015: Leading in the new world of work*, engagement is sighted as the single most important issue facing organisations today. Culture, engagement and leadership, previously viewed as *softer* areas, have become urgent priorities. I believe women are instrumental in reengineering workplace culture and leadership. After decades of short-term gain over long-term sustainable growth, we are seeing high turnover and disengagement. There is a greater demand for meaningful work with flexible conditions and a caring environment. At the core of women communicating with confidence in the workplace is having an opinion, upholding standards, sharing ideas, connecting people and caring about others while maintaining our identity.

How do we convey confidence in a way that's still feminine and assertive? I believe there are five areas to achieving this:

- **Believing we're enough as we are – we are equal, independent of titles and trappings**

- **Acknowledging our uniqueness** – being proud of our strengths and talents
- **Being open to listening** – not making it personal
- **Having the generosity to build up others** – especially other women
- **Having the courage to seek feedback** – when you're truly okay with who you are, feedback is a gift.

Building self-confidence is like building a muscle – it takes regular practice. Sometimes we might do more repetitions, other times less. We change our program because the activities that used to challenge us are now comfortable. When we don't exercise, or haven't in a while, new physical activity can feel challenging and uncomfortable. Building self-confidence is about giving it a go and having the strength to keep going beyond the discomfort.

There are steps you can take right now to improve your self-confidence muscle – consistent steps are key. This can be making a phone call that would usually make you feel uncomfortable, sharing your ideas in a group, nominating yourself for an award or applying for something you perhaps might not feel ready for yet. By doing small repeated actions and discovering you're still okay after each, you begin to build situation-based confidence, and in turn, self-confidence.

A technique I've used and continue to use in situations that are new or unknown, is to set my intention. To do this, I physically pause and ask myself, 'If I'm the most confident version of me, how am I behaving?'. From this mindset and context, I contribute to conversation, interact with others and present myself as the most confident version of me. The more times I've done this, the more confident I feel during interactions in unfamiliar situations. Overtime, it has become the new normal and what was previously, uncomfortable is no longer.

## Chapter One Practice

To build your confidence zone make the following a regular practice:

- **Get clear.** Pause for a moment somewhere quiet and set your intention: what's the purpose of this meeting/phone call/event/speech and what's my ideal outcome?
- **Get confident.** If you're feeling low on confidence, ask yourself, 'If I'm the most confident version of me right now, how am I being?' Alternatively, think of a confident person you admire and ask, 'If I was (insert name), how am I behaving in this situation?'.
- **Get leverage.** Identify two things you spend a large amount of time on. For example, writing reports, cleaning your house, organising your finances, shopping for clothes, social media maintenance, bookkeeping, etc. Look at delegating or outsourcing these tasks to someone who is more experienced, so you can do more of what you're best at.
- **Get perspective.** What are you afraid of right now? Take a moment, write down your answer. Now write down what you need to do specifically to change this. Place your answers somewhere you'll see them often.

## Your Chapter One Commitments:

What is one thing from this chapter you are committing to taking action on now?

(space for writing)

# 2
## Recalibration

*The ultimate truth of who you are is not, 'I am this' or 'I am that', but 'I Am'.*

~ Eckhart Tolle

We have a personal territory that goes beyond material possessions – our individuality. We are the sum of our beliefs, ethics, morals and philosophy. Our inner spark is what defines us as unique and separate to others. Recalibration is about shifting our source of self-worth from an external source to within, giving us ownership of the source for future fulfilment. Recalibration begins with developing the tools to trust our own thinking and judgement to overcome self-doubt.

Historically, strength was about fighting for survival and for territory. Now strength is about strength of character; standing up for our beliefs and being able to express these beliefs despite risking possible rejection in the process. Strength of character is maintaining our identity even when it doesn't conform to the groups you mix in. It can be tempting to conform to group expectations. By avoiding conflict and pleasing others, we feel safe. Strength is not stubbornness – it's self-expression without aggression. Individuality comes with consequences in the form of approval or disapproval from our environment. A strong character expresses freely, knowing there's a chance of receiving negative feedback and being okay with that.

As women, we generally care about what others think. We want to be liked and we notice when the opinion of another person is unfavourable. Ultimately, fulfilment comes from within, so when we're hooked on gaining praise to feel we're enough, we're giving away our control of feeling okay with who we are. Recalibration is about who we are and shifting our source of validation and self-worth from an external environment (others) to an internal environment (us). Sometimes the thought of letting others down is a stronger driving force, than standing up for our own preferences.

The distinction between personal excellence and striving for affection, depends on the standards we have for ourselves, compared to the standards expected by our environment. Are they based on our desire to be better at something, or not wanting to let others down? Striving for affection by doing excellent work, is analogous to chasing moving goal posts. Just when you score a goal, the goal posts shift or the rules of the game change. The short-term high is soon replaced by feelings of exhaustion. This creates a cycle of delivering personal excellence but not feeling certain about the quality of our work – what we were previously rewarded for continues to evolve. This is why feeling self-confident within is more powerful, more rewarding and more sustainable.

Confidence emanates from within. That's when we're at our most compelling and communicating with more clout. We gain an idea of how others perceive or experience us through their reactions, language and body language. This, in turn, affects how we see ourselves – it's the ultimate feedback loop.

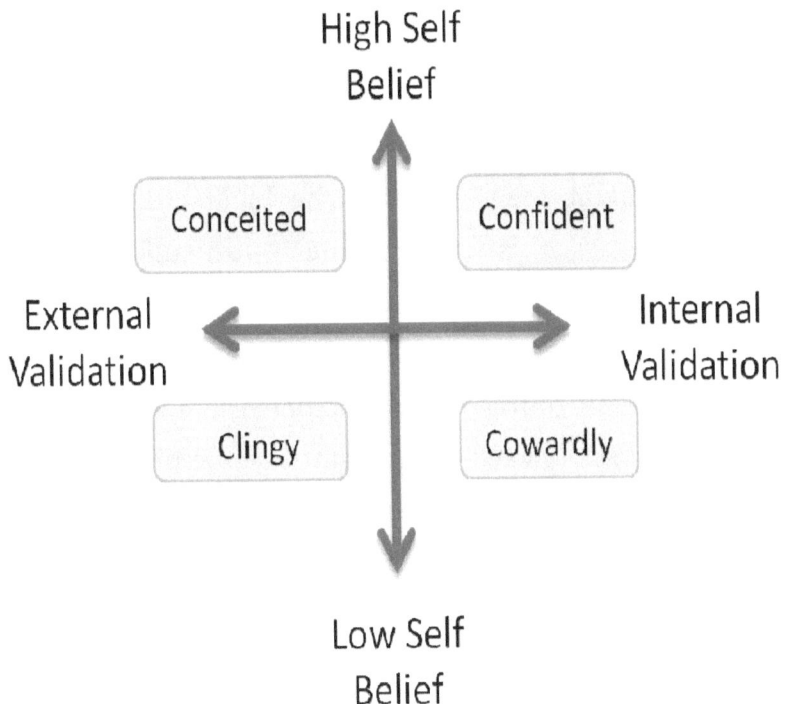

The confidence map provides an overview of how our self-belief and need for approval contribute to how we come across to others. A robust self-confidence supports our belief in our capability and ability to handle whatever comes our way. With robust self-confidence, our verbal and non-verbal language changes.

I believe it's possible to have an internal source of validation, but if your self-belief is low, you're more likely to shut down to avoid risk of possible criticism. A person who does this doesn't believe in themselves or their value. Similarly, a person with low self-belief who has a need for external approval and validation, may come across as clingy. They live in constant fear of not being good enough, which perpetuates a reliance on praise from others to feel okay. A need for external approval, combined with high self-belief, also contributes to a need for regular approval and feedback.

Internal validation provides us with inner calm and contentment. It brings a feeling of balance and equilibrium, even when our environment might seem chaotic. The biggest difference I've noticed within myself, is feeling calmer. I can still feel nervous about some things, but I'm anchored by a deeper sense of calm and acceptance – no matter what happens, I know I'll be okay. Self-worth provides courage to take bolder risks and make things happen. In contrast, low self-worth contributes to procrastination, because we're either waiting for permission or not wanting to take action that contributes to becoming more visible.

Growing up, the main sources of authority were our parents and our teachers. At primary school, we were rewarded for being compliant, following the rules, working diligently, colouring within the lines and not talking. For girls who are emotionally wired sooner, so they pick up on approval and emotional cues earlier, which is why women may be more likely to seek, or wait for permission before doing something out of the ordinary where there are no clear rules. High compliance does not always translate well in life beyond school, especially for women. I believe we've been conditioned to value following rules, more than thinking creatively or innovatively. Fortunately, this is changing.

When we feel we're enough, we're more motivated to try something new or approach a familiar activity in a different way. This cushions failure, as we're in control of our achievements and have a direct connection with effort and outcome. As long as we seek external feedback as our primary source of validation, we don't own our actions or results and will fear failure. I believe this is why internal validation is so important to gain success on your terms.

*No one can make you feel inferior without your consent.*
~ Eleanor Roosevelt

Expressions such as, 'fuelled from within' and 'lit from within' are great examples of recalibration. The question is, how do we shift self-worth if we're wired to seek feedback, praise and avoid criticism from the outside world? How do we internalise we're enough, despite years of feeling the opposite

Experiencing self-doubt is normal, because confidence is situational. Connecting with your confidence zone means reframing self-doubt within the context of the situation and shifting your focus to your belief that you'll deliver to the best of your ability.

Have you ever seen women trying on clothes and asking a shopping companion or sales assistant if they look okay? Perhaps you might have been this woman at some stage? They're bypassing their internal source of judgement and inviting someone else to be the authority. Move past this by always checking in with your own thoughts and feelings before asking someone else for theirs.

In this example above, even if we don't have great fashion sense, by forming an opinion first and then seeking input, we learn why our judgement might be off-track compared to a (usually) more highly trained eye. Without forming our opinion first, we miss the opportunity to refine our judgement and build competence and future confidence in this area.

Our differences are what make us unique. Only when we embrace what makes us different, will we truly be accepted by others for who we are. This is a lot less exhausting than keeping up with how we believe we need to be. It's an investment in self-worth. The alternative is being who we believe we need to be and being liked for this, which means never feeling accepted for who we really are.

I was born with very fair skin and grew up in the 70s when having a tan was all the rage. A deep bronze tan was *the* hot accessory to have – you couldn't escape it! It was highlighted in the media via advertisements for coconut oil, swimsuits, fashion, sunglasses and pictures of men and women drinking various beverages, all sporting glowing tanned skin. Adding to this was the way people spoke about having a tan: 'Oh, have you been on holidays? Wow, great tan!' or 'Oh, wow! You look fabulous with a tan!'.

I felt extremely self-conscious at the time. It seems trivial now, but it occupied my thoughts heavily, particularly during summer. I remember being invited to a pool party when I was twelve and the excitement soon gave way to feelings of inadequacies at the prospect of being in my bathers and revealing my ultra-fair skin. In my attempts to fit in and look the part, I experimented with self-tanning lotion. Back then, tanning lotions weren't as natural-looking as they are now. I ended up going to this party, feeling mortified, not because of my hang-up about my fair skin, but because I looked like a stripy carrot!

As well as my early athletics experiences, I worked in the fitness industry for a number of years. In this environment, it was expected (and still is, mostly) that instructors are lean and athletic, with tanned skin. The bronzed Aussie is a national icon. Buying into this ideal, I wore fake tan for over three years. I had a system down pat: exfoliate, apply my tanning lotion, then three days later exfoliate and reapply. I had a specific baggy black t-shirt, wore dark coloured pyjamas and slept on dark coloured sheets so you couldn't see the tan stains!

Shortly after leaving the industry, I decided I'd had enough of being who I wasn't and was tired of the high maintenance that went with using fake tan. So I went cold-turkey and by the end of the week, my natural skin colour had almost completely returned. I confess, I'd forgotten how fair I really was and it took some time to get used to it. Initially, I felt vulnerable and unattractive, like I did back when I was twelve. It wasn't until a male colleague made an off-hand comment, about my 'stunning fair skin', that I realised how deeply I had bought into the media's perception of what I thought I should look like.

That comment was the wakeup call I needed to realise my worth went beyond having a tan. Up until that moment, I'd never heard anyone describing fair skin as being something desirable, except with references to last century! My family used to joke that if I had been born a hundred years ago, my skin would have been a prized possession. I'm now proudly an ambassador for sunscreen!

External standards of attractiveness have changed. We've seen Audrey Hepburn, Twiggy, Marilyn Monroe, Elle McPherson and Naomi Campbell as poster pinups for what an attractive woman looks like. Yet, these women are all very different in appearance.

The more I've embraced my differences, the more content I've become with myself and who I am as a person. It's our differences that make us more interesting, more memorable and also more open to feedback – good, bad or otherwise.

Behaviours such as consistently not meeting deadlines or not taking responsibility to complete tasks, can sometimes be a product of not having much opportunity to test boundaries as a child. With boundaries come opportunities for confidence-building. Our well-intending parents or role models may have rescued us to keep us safe, or completed a regular activity as a favour (e.g., homework), or perhaps not held us to the same standards as other siblings.

When I was growing up, I wasn't allowed to have a bike. I used to think that was terribly unfair because my brother was given a bike for his birthday. I asked why I wasn't allowed to have one and was given responses such as, 'It's not safe'. I believe it was my parent's way of preventing me from falling off or falling over – all those things that you learn when riding a bike. When a child never experiences consequences of falling off a bike, or not getting homework in on time, they don't develop the responsibility needed to perform the task, build competence and, in turn, confidence.

Last summer I was at a park playground with my kids, watching them as they climbed up and down the play equipment. Standing close by were well-intentioned grandparents with their young grandson. When the child began an activity such as climbing, going down the slide, or balancing, he was told, 'Don't do that, you'll fall!' or 'Don't do that, you'll hurt yourself!'. It left me wondering what impact consistent messages such as these during childhood have on developing self-confidence later in life.

## Chapter Two Practice

To build your sense of internal validation, make the following a regular practice:

- **Get clear.** What's important to you right now that you've not taken action on yet, because you're concerned about what others may think? What does your career look like when you take action?
- **Get confident.** Think back to a time when you over-prepared for something work related. How has the need to over-prepare played out in your life so far? What is this costing you? How are your results different when you let go of the need to please others?
- **Get leverage.** If you want to feel worthy, behave as if you are worthy. Respect yourself and others (no more water cooler talk and idle gossip). Our actions and the way we treat ourselves teaches others how to treat us. Speak about others as if they are standing next to you – even when they aren't.
- **Get perspective.** Now that you're aware of the difference between internal and external validation, write down what feedback means to you now.

## Your Chapter Two Commitments:

What is one thing from this chapter you are committing to taking action on now?

_____
_____
_____
_____
_____
_____
_____
_____
_____
_____
_____
_____
_____

# 3
# Mini Me

*Change your thinking, change your life.*

~ Ernest Holmes

We have complete control over our thoughts. Yes, that's right! Our thinking is under our direct control and no one else is planting thoughts in our minds – yet!

Our thinking shows up as self-talk. According to Dr Athena Staik in her article, *Toxic Thinking Patterns*, 'our thoughts or "self-talk" are an inner running commentary, a stream of about 60,000 thoughts a day.' Self-talk is sometimes kind and encouraging. More often, it's the voice of the inner critic (blame, fault-finding, self-pity, etc.) and it can be loud at times! These are not real thoughts; they're a reflection of deeper limiting beliefs, according to Dr Staik. The voice of our inner critic is a barometer of self-worth. I believe the quality of our life is proportional to the quality of our thinking, which makes getting a handle on self-talk a priority. I believe this is a contributing factor to the popularity of mindfulness, and creating space to acknowledge our thoughts without reacting to them.

Mindset is a major contributor to achieving results. The 400m sprint story I shared during the introduction was an example of how we can experience different results with a mindset that's working *for us*, not against us. Health and fitness have remained a constant theme in my life, not because I'm naturally gifted or athletic, but because health is a core value for me and I've cultivated an effective mindset to deliver results in this area of my life.

I discovered aerobics in the 80s and became an aerobics groupie. I loved attending classes, the beat of the music, the routines and dare I say it – the fashion! I also discovered aerobics competitions and after attending my first as a spectator, I was hooked! I decided competition was something I wanted to do and more than this – had to do. Soon after, my boyfriend at the time was offered a great career opportunity overseas. I decided this was a blessing in disguise and an opportunity to focus on my dream.

The moment I decided to compete was also the moment I decided I wanted to win. I *chose* to believe I could win. I had no prior experience apart from regularly attending aerobics classes. After researching mentors, I was ecstatic to find Sue Stanley, a three-times world champion, based in Maidstone, Melbourne. I called her up, we met and she agreed to train me. I began my journey training six days a week, two to three hours each day, in addition to my corporate job. It became a lifestyle and rewarding experience to bond with a fantastic group of people, united by a shared dream of competing (and winning!). Through this experience I learned the mindset to achieve a sports outcome is similar to achieving a business outcome.

Here's my ten-step gold medal strategy:

1. **Get clear on your compelling reason to take action**
2. **Make a decision and fully commit**
3. **Seek out a mentor**
4. **Do what your mentor tells you to the best of your ability (know your benchmarks to measure progress)**
5. **Stay curious**
6. **Research and model excellence**
7. **Bring your passion**
8. **Meditate each day on achieving your goal, specifically: how it feels, what steps you've taken to get there, what resources you used, and where you needed to improve. See yourself achieving, feel yourself achieving and notice what you can hear when you do**
9. **Master your thoughts – minimise or reframe unhelpful thinking**
10. **Back yourself every day.**

How do you rate the self-talk you experience each day? Are the comments positive? Are they mostly neutral? Or are they negative? A mixture of all three is normal; it's about balance and the proportion of each.

When the majority of comments are a form of self-criticism, judgement or putdown, it becomes even easier to access further negative thinking and thought patterns. The quality of our thinking and self-talk is a barometer of our relationship with ourselves. The great news is, it's also a *choice* and can be changed as quickly as we want. The challenge comes with the decision to want to change the quality of your thinking and the discipline to do this each day.

What are most of your with others conversations about? Are they mainly about people and who did what? How about what's wrong with your workplace, relationships or what's going on in general? Alternatively, are your conversations about ideas, possibilities and finding solutions? Pause for a moment and reflect on how you feel energetically during the different styles of conversation mentioned. Which style engages you, which style do you find most interesting and which style is most inspiring? You've had conversations where you will have experienced all of these.

In a nutshell: people who have a tendency to consistently steer the conversation towards the negative, become socially undesirable, and no fun to be around. The energy we bring to our physical space is a reflection of our attitude and mindset.

What's the calibre of conversation going on in your head? How do you feel during this chatter? Minimising negative self-talk or self-criticism is important. When we do, we feel less anxious and experience less self-doubt. Overcoming self-doubt is about believing we're enough and not buying into who we think the world wants us to be.

Self-confidence is an attitude, it's a way of approaching the world, and it changes how we experience life each day. Our self-esteem is based on our perception of other people's judgement of us. By treating other people as if they like you already, you're creating a foundation for instant rapport building rather than a sanitised polite greeting.

Years ago I read a book on customer service. A suggestion made in this book, was to greet people as if they're your best friend –

so I tried it. At the time, I was working in private practice and decided to road test this when I greeted my clients. Each time, just before walking into the waiting area, I paused for a moment, thought about my best friend and the fun times we have together. As soon as I immersed in the feeling, I walked into the waiting room and greeted each client with a beaming smile. Wow, it made a noticeable difference! Not only was there was rapid rapport, deeper connection and more fun, I seemed to enjoy our appointment time together even more.

People respond to how you're being more than what you're doing. Whether you come from a place of warmth or a place of judgement, it's contagious. If all we have in our head is self-judgement, people pick up on micro expressions and the corresponding energy we give off. Have you ever walked into a quiet room and felt tension or uneasiness in the air? Energy accompanies the emotional state we're in and its palpable.

Think back to when you met someone for the first time – a networking event for example. What was energy like of the people you met? Did other people seem mostly warm and friendly towards you, or hesitant and reserved? Is this experience consistent with other experiences? Intuitively, we pick up the energy of people around us – their *vibe* – and this contributes to how socially desirable we feel and what we believe to be true about us. It can become a self-fulfilling prophecy.

In Sharon Begley's book, *Train Your Mind, Change Your Brain*, Begley discusses how experiments in neuroplasticity have revealed the brain is capable of altering its structure and function well into old age. This means we can build new thought habits essential to rewiring our brain to enhance our mindset. If you haven't already, when is now a great time to start? When we change our habitual ways of thinking, we create physical changes in our brain which can override genetics and change brain chemistry. Through this, we develop greater emotional resilience and feel more content within ourselves.

When you wake in the morning, what's the very first thing to go through your mind? Take yourself back to this morning and replay the thinking and self-talk that framed up your day. Were your thoughts mostly positive, mostly negative or a mixture? A positive thought pattern might go something like this: (alarm goes off) 'How cosy is this bed, hmm what day is it? ... It's Tuesday, I get to present the Davidson Report today. Can't wait to finally do this, after weeks of work. I'm flattered to have the opportunity to do this. I'm going to present this incorporating Sue's feedback from yesterday – I think that will work well. Let's do this!'

In contrast, for someone who is disengaged with their career, job or business, their thought pattern might go something like this: (alarm goes off) 'Oh, god, not the alarm. I'm so tired. I can't believe it's time to get up already ... It's too cold outside. What day is it? It's Tuesday. The damn Davidson Report is today. It's taken sooo long to complete this and it's probably a waste of time anyway. And bloody Sue wants it done her way after only telling me yesterday that I should change it! I hate being told what to do. Why can't she do the presentation if she's the expert? I don't know why they keep asking me to do the presentations; it means I have to do more work than everyone else in the team. I hope I don't freeze up like I did last time; that was horrible, everyone staring at me and I didn't know what to say, I better bring handout photocopies just in case. Damn, Cheryl never sent the final draft back so I don't know if she made those last minute changes. Why does Cheryl have to take so long? It's like she moves in slow motion ... Oh crap, time to get up!'.

What do you notice about the two examples above? The first is shorter, with a clearer focus, calmness and certainty about the day. The second has longer dialogue and is building up momentum. In this last example, momentum could be fuelled by walking into the bathroom, not liking the reflection in the mirror, noticing mess around the house, being in heavy traffic or not having a train arrive on time – you get the message.

For many women, the inner voice in their head is rarely the voice of praise or of affirmation. Continuing to immerse your mind in negative thoughts, creates a feedback loop, transforming negative neural pathways into neural highways. This makes it even easier to access negative thought patterns. Like tyres in a dirt track, the grooves they make become deeper and deeper each time they go down the path. Over time, it becomes more difficult to avoid the grooves and make a separate track.

After learning about this fact, I decided to experiment with this. For an entire day I committed to maintaining positive or neutral self-talk. As soon as I recognised inner voice commentary that was negative, I reframed this into either a neutral or a positive statement where possible. Like a commentator, I generated an ongoing stream of internal conversation throughout the day. It was mentally exhausting! Interestingly, at the end of it, I felt different. My mind hadn't been exposed to the same volume of negative conversation. Instead, I felt calmer, more grounded and more positive.

The way we think of ourselves creates a separate world in our head. This world is a unique ecosystem, a unique mix of our values, beliefs, attitudes, and understandings. These form filters for how we experience daily life, because our thoughts have already passed through these filters without us being aware.

> *Great minds discuss ideas, average minds discuss events and small minds discuss people.*
>
> ~ Eleanor Roosevelt

How do we go about changing our inner voice if it's not helping us grow and evolve? The goal is to either turn down its volume, (not remove it) or reframe the conversation. Once we accept the voice will always be there, we need to find a way to manage it. Turning down its volume dial until it becomes background noise, gives us the choice to listen or not.

In Dr Staik's *Toxic Thinking* article, she describes habitual thinking patterns that cause intense feelings of fear, anger, shame or guilt are toxic and addictive in nature. According to Dr Staik, we're addicted because, paradoxically, this type of thinking stimulates the pleasure and learning centres – similar to addictive substances. Interestingly, in the presence of fear (real or perceived), our brain is at its most alert and most receptive to learning.

In the article, *The Complexity of Fear,* Mary Lamia PhD describes fear as a survival mechanism for protecting humans from threats, in earlier times. We paid attention to what was different in our surroundings, we noticed anything that was different and we aimed to fit in and be accepted by the tribe. Being different meant standing out, which was a potential threat to our safety and decreased our chances of survival if the tribe rejected us.

When our mind is bombarded by information and conversation that's mostly negative and/or judgemental, our world becomes negative and judgemental. How we experience our life is a reflection of how we experience our thinking. The first step to any change is becoming aware of the conversation we're having in our head.

An effective way of lowering the volume of your inner critic is by reducing the negative stimuli, triggers and negative conversations around you as well as within you. They both contribute to the total volume of information we take in each day. A good example of negative conversation in the environment is the news on television.

My perception is that there seems to be less good news stories talked about on TV and radio these days, compared to thirty years ago. For this reason, I don't watch the news. Taking this a step further, I made a conscious decision over four years ago not to watch *any* television at all. It's been a fascinating journey! What I've noticed is, despite avoiding exposure to what was previously a substantial volume of dialogue (budget cuts, political slinging matches, bombings, stabbings, rapes, killings, celebrity drama – you get the point), I'm still aware of what's going on in the world. How is this possible? Television is only *one* source of information. We're bombarded with thousands of messages each day from a range of mediums.

For example, I walked past a newsagent and saw a promotional board with a headline stating musician, Prince, had passed away. Sources such as this are how we can still be aware of what's going on, but not be in a position to have an in-depth conversation on the subject.

Another source of top line information is in cafes or restaurants, anywhere people might be reading the paper. At these venues, you'll often see the front page of a newspaper that's sitting next to the counter while waiting for a coffee, or at the table next to you while someone is reading their daily news. There might be a radio station playing the news in the background. There are ads on the sides of trams about upcoming events and shows. Sometimes you may find you're listening to the news while on hold on the phone, or see magazine headlines while standing in line at the checkout. It's amazing what information we absorb despite choosing to not to tune into television or radio.

Much of my current affairs knowledge comes from reading online articles and blogs. There is regular commentary based on what's happening in the world featured in these, and I find them to be more constructive and more interesting. The strategy I've shared with you here, is how I've managed to turn down the volume of negative dialogue in my environment. I appreciate this approach won't immediately appeal to some readers, but for those who want to experience feeling more grounded, calmer and more productive, I highly recommend having a go!

The other effective strategy for quietening negative self-talk is making regular space for thoughts of gratitude. I don't mean being grateful in a detached manner. Instead, immersing in the feeling – even for just sixty seconds each day.

We can all manage one minute – it's up to you to decide and exercise the discipline.

Recently, the ducted heating played up, so instead having a toasty warm house in the morning, it felt icy cold. It was also the day I had blocked out to write at home (hot tip: if you don't schedule it, it doesn't happen!). For the entire day, I huddled at my computer, wearing many layers and feeling the cool air on my face and hands. Yes, I could have gone to the library, or a friend's house, but the quiet environment was important for me to focus. Later that night when the heating was fixed, I felt physical relief and gratitude for the privilege of having the ducted heating working, and also grateful for the standard of living we have in Australia, compared to third world nations. It's the physical sensation that comes with gratitude, that's important for this approach to work.

Gratitude is a very powerful thought process. During my coaching studies, I learned we can't experience love and trust at the same time as experiencing fear and doubt. If it's true that these emotions cannot exist simultaneously, then as long as we feel fear and/or self-doubt, our ability to experience love and trust is diminished. Each night, as my head hits the pillow, I think of five things I'm grateful for that happened during my day. These can be simple things, like seeing a beautiful sunrise that morning, the smile on my children's faces when they look at me or a kind gesture from someone. When we practice gratitude, even for brief moments, we strengthen our neurological pathways for positive thoughts, creating shifts in our brain chemistry.

Practicing gratitude is easy. I began an evening mealtime practice of 'highlights'. My kids are too young to fully understand the concept of gratitude so we talk about one thing we enjoyed during the day. If you prefer to use a diary, write down what you're grateful for each day in there. Over time, you'll create a collection of things you're grateful for, which becomes an effective resource to revisit, whenever you're having a low energy moment or low energy day.

Regular meditation is another way of taming unruly negative self-talk. My biggest misconception about meditation was that it had to be for at least half an hour, ideally an hour, a day. This is completely untrue. There's no definitive statement on how long a meditation needs to be; rather, it's the consistency of creating space for thoughts to flow – free from judgement.

## Chapter Three Practice

To experience better self-talk, make the following a regular practice:

- **Get clear.** Do your own thinking assessment. Select a thirty-minute block on a non-work day and rate your thoughts during this time. On a piece of paper, add a tick, a cross or a circle to show if the thought was positive, negative or neutral. The content of your thoughts is not important, it's the ratio of positive to negative that's valuable to have awareness of.
- **Get confident.** Grab a notepad and pen and place it beside your bed. Each night before falling asleep *or* each morning before getting out of bed, record one thing you are proud of.
- **Get leverage.** Greet others as if they're your best friend.

- **Get perspective. Embrace a low-information diet for one week. No television, radio or social media. Yes, you will survive! Notice the differences in your head space at the end of that week. How do you feel? How is this different to your normal headspace?**

## Your Chapter Three Commitments:

What is one thing from this chapter you are committing to taking action on now?

(space for writing)

_____

_____

_____

_____

_____

_____

_____

_____

# 4
## Multiple Dimensions

*Today you are you, that is truer than true. There is no one alive, who is more youer than you!*

~ Dr Seuss

The closest we come to knowing who we really are is deciding on our core values. By defining the principles we defend and the philosophies we subscribe to, we're able to define ourselves more clearly.

What I've found is that most people don't really know who they are at their core. We grow up being exposed to millions of marketing messages and images promoting what we should have, who we should be and how we should look. Ironically, our adult life can be a journey of unlearning who we think we should be and exploring who we really are. The great news is, we can change what we don't like and the first step to personal growth begins with self-awareness.

Self-awareness and self-acceptance are the core foundation blocks for building self-confidence. *Knowing* who we are, *embracing* who we are and *being* who we are, is a journey. We will only truly feel like we belong when we accept who we are and share our authentic self with others. If we continue to be who we think our family, colleagues, or community want us to be, we miss out on experiencing the gift of true acceptance.

Years of research on personality has identified five core traits of personality – coined the 'Big Five' by American personality psychologist, Lewis Goldberg. This theory was developed as a complete overview of dimensions or traits that make up our personality – to predict thoughts, feelings and actions. In a review of the Big Five personality traits by Psychosocial Rehabilitation Specialist, Kendra Cherry, the five dimensions of personality are represented as a range along a continuum between extremes. The five factors are:

- **Extraversion – sociability, talkativeness, emotional expressiveness**
- **Agreeableness – Trust, kindness, affection**
- **Conscientiousness – self-discipline, cautiousness, orderliness**
- **Neuroticism – emotional instability, moodiness, sadness**
- **Openness – creativity, imagination, insight**

In her article *The Big Five Personality Traits*, Cherry highlights that behaviour involves an interaction between both underlying personality and situational variables. Each dimension of personality plays a role in adapting our situational behaviour.

To bring these dimensions to life, think of stereotyped personas. For example: teacher, warrior, clown, seductress, rebel, child, nurturer, sage or royalty – each has a repertoire of typical or expected behaviours. Our ability to access different dimensions and behave in ways to express these appropriately, shows behavioural flexibility. Behavioural flexibility is part of emotional flexibility.

Think of someone you know who is really funny, a natural at witty jokes and who sees the lighter side of any occasion. Imagine being at a dinner with this person – they're entertaining, enjoyable to be around and perhaps the life of the party. Imagine the same humorous conversation played out in a different context, such as at a funeral or a parent teacher night. The same jokes are most likely to be seen as inappropriate during these occasions. The context changes the desirability of behaviours.

Based on her research into personality and mindset, Stanford psychologist, Professor Carol Dweck, suggests our ability to change our personality depends on whether we have a *fixed* or a *growth* mindset. In the article, *Fixed vs. Growth: The Two Basic Mindsets That Shape Our Lives*, Professor Dweck describes a *fixed* mindset, as believing our personality is static (for example: 'that's just the way I am'). Our intelligence is finite and our moral character fixed. This mindset is associated with less behavioural flexibility. In contrast, a *growth* mindset is based on a belief that our personality is the starting point for development, giving us the ability to cultivate our qualities through applied effort and experience. So while personality traits may evolve over time with concerted effort and a *growth* mindset, our behaviour adapts rapidly according to the situation. I believe to feel accepted, we need to display consistency in personality and adaptability of behaviour.

I believe all personas (teacher, warrior, clown, seductress, rebel, child, nurturer, sage or royalty), exist within each of us. As we grow-up and explore the behaviours of different personas in different situations, we learn which seem to work more effectively and which seem to suit who we believe we are. We're capable of accessing all personas, but typically develop a preference for two or three of these. This is also where we find the origin of our confidence zone.

From the list below, select which of the following you relate to the *most* in a work environment:

- **I prefer to be calling the shots, achieving goals and taking action**
- **I prefer to be having fun, being around other people and being spontaneous**
- **I prefer to be helping others, having clear instructions and being organised**
- **I prefer to be an expert at what I do, assess the fine print before making a decision and provide valuable critical thinking**

You might relate to all of these on some level. The questions worth exploring are: which one do you relate to more? Are there two that seem to resonate equally for you? Do you prefer the focus of your work to be on people, tangible things, systems or conceptual thinking? How is this a match for your current work environment?

The purpose of this activity is to expand your self-awareness around your preferred work style and if necessary, look at how you can modify your current situation to better suit your preferred way of working. We do our best work, in an environment that supports our work style preferences, which means we can consistently perform in our zone of confidence.

The personas we're most comfortable with become our default behaviours. Building behavioural flexibility means accessing different personas, even the ones that make us feel uncomfortable. For example, if you've ever received feedback about speaking up more, that's an indication you're not accessing your more dominant personas. With behavioural flexibility comes the ability to speak up, communicate with impact and be heard. This contributes to building self-confidence.

When I was twelve, I discovered how powerful immersing myself in the mental and emotional state of another person can be. It was a Sunday night, Dad was going to be home late from a day trip and Mum, my brother Peter, and I were eating dinner together at the table. We usually didn't have the television on during dinner, but on this occasion we did and *60 Minutes* was on the screen in the background. The reporters were interviewing a young woman who had survived a brutal stabbing attack. I was morbidly fascinated and wondered what such an ordeal must have been like. It seemed incredible that a person could have survived so much. In detail, I did my best to visualise and internalise what she might have experienced, both mentally and physically. The next thing I remember, was waking up on the floor – I had passed out! This was to be another clue in the power of mindset.

Last year, I was assisting to facilitate a training session. Part of this training was focussed on accessing different personas and role playing the corresponding behaviours. There was a young woman with a kind and caring nature in the class. She spoke softly and exuded a feminine energy. In the training, she was given the challenge of playing out the behaviours of a persona that was far removed from her own gentle nature – the warrior persona. She did her best to find her inner warrior. For the others in the room waiting their turn, they could see her behaviour was not very convincing. The art of mastering this challenge is to immerse in the thinking and physical energy of the persona assigned to you. This creates behavioural flexibility and a boost to self-confidence. For most people, this is a defining moment they cherish as they access a part of themselves that's normally buried or shut down.

After much repetition and time, we celebrated our newly crowned warrior. In the process, she had amplified her power range and added behavioural flexibility to her repertoire. She had also created new neural pathways to access the thinking needed and the corresponding physical energy. In times when we need to bring focus, drive and persistence your warrior persona and energy is perfect for this!

No matter how much we know or understand the logic, we cannot truly access a persona until we take on the thinking and filters (attitudes, values and beliefs) that go with it. This is the difference between a great actress and an average one. The ABC Model of Attitudes, reviewed by Saul McLeod, describes how a person's behaviour is expected to be consistent with the attitudes they hold, according to *the principle of consistency*. Attitudes affect the way we live, the choices we make and our emotions associated with strong beliefs – such as religious or political views.

The pattern I continue to see in women I work with, is a shared limiting belief that being assertive is the same as being aggressive. They also believe if they're assertive they will lose their femininity and friends. Being soft and nice all the time is not always going to lead to better relationships or results. There are times when we need to have difficult conversations, be direct, set firm boundaries or standards and uphold them. If we don't, we're not taken seriously and risk being taken advantage of. Clients, customers and children appreciate clear messages and expectations.

*The problem is never the problem! It is only a symptom of something much deeper.*

~ Virginia Satir

The warrior persona and energy is a great example of a powerful emotional state and inner resource for when you want to achieve something, or move beyond your comfort zone. Do we need to be channelling this energy all the time? No, and I advise against it! Through taking action, taking on things that are outside our comfort zone, we grow, boost our confidence, increase self-confidence and become who we *really* are.

And as a parent of two young children, this is particularly relevant. Children thrive when they feel safe and secure, and they feel this when having consistent boundaries for things that are important. As an example in our household: we have very clear boundaries for the amount of screen time the kids are allowed each day. Early on, the boundaries were tested. With consistent reinforcement, this didn't last long. Now, we can leave the iPads out and the kids will not use them until it's screen time later in the afternoon.

When we're clear on our strengths and stretches, we're empowered to proactively manage our personal and professional growth. A distinction on strengths and stretches: strengths are things we're comfortable with, good at and can do well more easily than others; stretches are activities that are less familiar, that we're not as good at and take us longer to do to. They're our less preferred way of behaving. Whilst our strengths give us power – and that's ultimately how we achieve our results – our stretches also represent an opportunity for growth. There are times when it's very valuable to work on our stretches and times when delegating these is a preferred option.

One of my personal stretches is being an Agony Aunt when the other person wants to have a lengthy vent. I define lengthy vents as more than ten-minutes long. Short vents of frustration are fine and I'm an advocate for short bursts to vent frustrations. However, when I hear the same complaints repeated again and again in subsequent conversations, my default tendency is to become very direct, ask what steps they've taken to remedy this and offer to brainstorm solutions or suggest we talk about something else.

In contrast, some women are great at playing the Agony Aunt role. You can ring them any time of day and they'll sit patiently and supportively, nodding and agreeing with you and making you feel comfortable. This is an example of different default personas and corresponding behaviours in action. Even when it's not my preferred way of behaviour, I can still choose to be the supportive comforter. It becomes a choice.

Without growth, we become stagnant. We have a fundamental need to grow, which is why I believe education continues beyond the formalised education years. As a society, we're the most educated we've ever been, yet we're also most obese, medicated, addicted and in debt we've ever been. Knowledge and education are not enough to thrive.

Why is this? Humans have a need for connection, yet it seems the more connected we've become via technology, the less connected we've become with ourselves. I believe in a world where likes and tweets impact self-confidence, the temptation is to post the best version of us – a *filtered* version of us. I believe part of this contributes to the disconnection some people feel.

Have you ever been out at a restaurant and seen two people who appear to be on a date, both on their phones? I'm concerned about the impact of this behaviour on communication skills and the relationships of future generations.

We can really only connect with and embrace another person as much as we embrace ourselves. Only when we love ourselves and who we are, can we deeply love another and who they are. How much we embrace who we are, feel valuable and feel we're enough is measured by self-worth. If we only love parts of us but not others, our self-worth is less than if we accept us as a complete package – acknowledging strengths, stretches and differences.

How do we develop a deeper sense of self-worth? The first step is by getting clear on our values. The term 'values' has been used quite a bit in recent years and the term seems to have become viewed as outdated. When you think about your life so far and the areas you've had the greatest results, you'll notice they're all related to the things you care about, and are most likely closely aligned with your highest values.

During childhood, we're asked questions by well-intentioned adults, such as, 'What do you want to be when you grow up?'. The assumption underlying this question is what we do, defines who we are and our role defines our identity. It's not surprising that some Year 12 students experience angst around deciding which subjects to do in their final years and what their next steps are beyond secondary school.

In a Changing Minds article, sociologist Morris Massey, describes three key periods when our values develop. Early childhood years up to the age of seven are the imprint years, where we absorb and accept much of the information around us, especially from parents or main care-givers. We take on their belief systems about what is right and wrong, good or bad, contributing a blueprint for our identity.

Following this, are the modelling years. From ages eight to thirteen, we try on the behaviours and attitudes of our parents, teachers and the people we look up to. I once heard a saying, 'we become who we most admired at the age of ten'. I don't know if there's any truth in this, but it does provide an interesting perspective to assess the decisions and actions we've made in our life to date. From ages thirteen to twenty-one, we're strongly influenced by peers, developing social relationships and social values.

Beyond the age of twenty-one our core values don't change significantly. The exception is with major emotional events or intensive coaching – creating shifts in thinking and a more resourceful mindset. Our core values are important as they drive our decisions and actions, and are consistent with the results we experience in life. For example, if health is a core value we'll prioritise health, make decisions and take action that consistently moves us toward better health. While our core values remain the same, our secondary values will change and grow over time according to what we're experiencing in life.

We become the leaders in areas where our highest values lie. We set the standard, we maintain the standard, and we become a role model to others in these areas. A value can be important to us, but it's our *highest values* that determine where we achieve our best results. For example, if your work is aligned with your values and it's something you care about, your days are fulfilling and rewarding, and you're much more likely to be achieving or moving towards great results.

Another way of expanding self-awareness, is by using profiling tools. There are a range of behavioural profiling tools, personality profiling tools and thinking profiling tools. My suggestion is to find and do as many as you can, because they each provide perspective and insight into different dimensions of you. Some of my preferred tools are: Extended DISC™, Strengths Finder 2.0™, How to Fascinate® and the Meta Dynamics™ Profiling tool.

Extended DISC™ is a behaviour profiling tool, completed online. The report generated, provides insights into our preferred behaviours and how these plays out in relationships, the workplace and how we respond under stress. Strengths Finder 2.0™ is a book which contains a link where you can complete the online assessment tool. The report assesses your natural strengths, providing insights into the types of roles we're well suited to. How To Fascinate® is another online assessment tool using the principles of advertising and influence and applies this to human behaviour. Your report explores how the world sees you at your best and how you fascinate others. The Meta Dynamics™ profiling tool uses four dimensions of human behaviour known as the Critical Alignment Model. This profiling tool gives you an easy to follow, step-by-step map for identifying where you are right now, how you can improve and ways to develop.

Being clear about your unique talents contributes to personal and professional fulfilment. When you're utilising your talents in way that connects you with meaningful work (something you care about), you'll feel more connected with a sense of contribution. This is a recipe for more rewarding work and relationships, as well as being a better parent, friend and partner.

## Chapter Four Practice

To build your self-awareness, make the following a regular practice:

- **Get clear.** Create a self-discovery journal – a book specifically to record your thoughts, learns and reflections.
- **Get confident.** Complete as many profiling tools as you can. What are you learning about you? What surprises you? Write these in your journal too.
- **Get leverage.** Write down a goal that lifts you up, inspires and excites you.
- **Get perspective.** Complete the Values Elicitation Activity. This can be found at the back of the book, in the Resources section. This activity will help you to become more aware of what matters to you. Add these to your discovery journal.

## Your Chapter Four Commitments:

What is one thing from this chapter you are committing to taking action on now?

(space for writing)

_____

_____

_____

_____

_____

_____

_____

_____

_____

_____

# PART TWO

# POWER

# 5
# Compelling Communication

*If you want me to speak for two minutes, it will take me three weeks of preparation. If you want me to speak for thirty minutes, it will take me a week to prepare. If you want me to speak for an hour, I am ready now.*

~ Winston Churchill

Compelling communication is about tapping into our power base – how we get results. Compelling communication is communicating effectively and with conviction. It's being able to cut through the noise with confidence, credibility and congruence.

Human beings are social animals and we're hard-wired to communicate and connect with others. In Gareth Cook's article, *Why We Are Wired to Connect,* he shares how our well-being, depends on our connections with others. Cook goes on to comment that humans have an unparalleled ability to cooperate and collaborate with others.

We want our communication to convey our message clearly with confidence and in a way that's congruent with our character. This may lead to professional development opportunities, leadership roles, future collaborations or more flexible work arrangements. Compelling communication is about using empowered language. Language that's not driven by a need to people please, be apologetic or downplay our best qualities and contributions.

One way we communicate self-doubt is through patterns in our speech. Women with undermining speech habits often do so subconsciously in order to appear likeable, friendly and non-threatening. Two of the most commonly used undermining speech habits include apologies (saying sorry automatically without emotional concern) and the use of minimisers (where women put themselves down or make themselves smaller with their words).

There is a phenomenon that women are perceived as either competent or likeable, but not both at the same time. In the Harvard Business Review article, *For Women Leaders, Likability and Success Hardly Go Hand-in-Hand*, female leaders were disliked more than men. I've personally seen women opting for likeable over competent and I've done this at times myself over the years! Paradoxically, in another Harvard Business Review article, *New Research Shows Success Doesn't Make Women Less Likeable*, authors Zenger and Folkman, conclude people like effective leaders who produce superior results, independent of gender. Which means, likeability and success can happily co-exist for women.

Many women tend to have a knack for diplomacy. I acknowledge there are some wonderfully diplomatic men too. In a general sense, women bring a quality of inclusion to the work environment. Sometimes women avoid taking a stand or sharing their opinion. In conversations with female clients and colleagues, they've confided that they sometimes feel held back. They question the value of their comment or they're concerned with the need to be right, so they opt to stay quiet, rather than be seen to be wrong. Have a think about the women around you. How likely are they to take a stand in a group setting, where there's a difference of opinion?

It's general knowledge that waiting for someone to finish speaking before you begin is considered polite and a sign of respect. From what I've observed during polite conversation, most women will share their ideas and thinking, as long as their comments don't impact their desire to be liked.

I grew up in an era where the saying, 'sugar and spice and all things nice' was common. I even had this printed on a t-shirt when I was five! Nice girls sat quietly, they didn't interrupt when others were speaking and in the presence of greater authority, they didn't speak unless spoken to, or they sought permission. It's not surprising my school reports frequently said, 'Kerryn is quiet and conscientious, but she needs to ask more questions and speak up more in class.' I appreciate how it feels when you experience internal resistance to speaking out.

If you relate to this, start small. Build practice by speaking up more in lower-stake environments and make a commitment to ask at least one question for every meeting you attend. Commit to this and it does become easier over time.

There are times to be passive and times to speak up. I believe women benefit in the long-term by speaking up during robust conversation where there may be differences of opinion, rather than waiting until afterwards and pulling someone aside in the hallway to say what they wanted to say during the meeting. Some women feel they're walking a fine line between speaking their truth without coming across as too direct or confronting. For professional women, business women and women who contribute to our communities, compelling communication is an essential skill to have.

## 3 SPHERES OF SELF CONFIDENCE

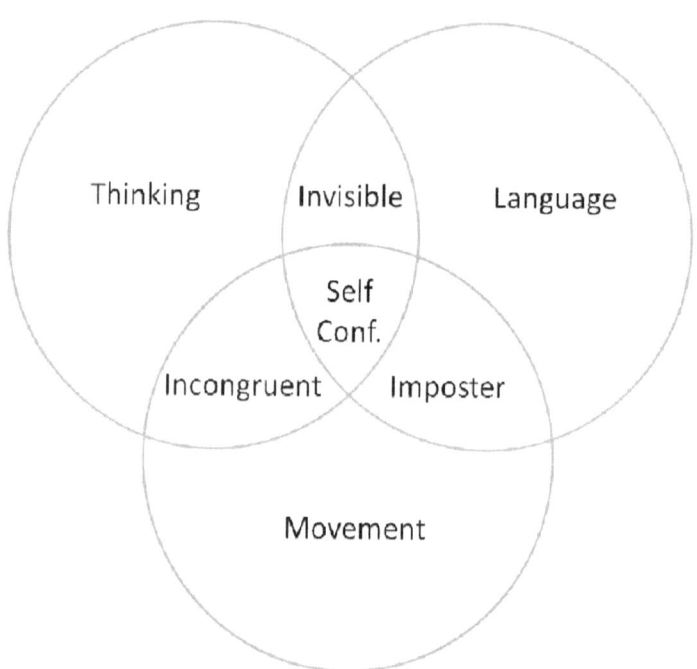

I believe self-confidence comes from a combination of three areas: thinking, language and movement. The first sphere, *thinking*, underpins all three. This sphere relates to our personal beliefs and convictions about the value we contribute.

Even with great language and movement, without the thinking, we feel like an imposter.

The second sphere, *language*, focuses on confidence, certainty in expression, the use of softeners (e.g., using words like 'perhaps' or 'might') and minimisers (e.g., using the word 'just') where appropriate. If we have the thinking and the movement but not language, we communicate incongruence and this detracts from our credibility.

The final sphere, *movement*, looks at the way women use their physicality to communicate confidence (e.g., the way we sit, stand, or present ourselves). We may have confident thinking and confident language, but without appropriate physical movement to support these, I believe we're at risk of being invisible (e.g., if we sit with closed detached body language, don't take action and share our thoughts). In her book, *Lean In: Women, Work and the Will to Lead*, Sheryl Sandberg shares how she observed women sitting in seats around the edge of the room during business meetings, despite there being enough chairs at the meeting table. Consequently, these women were more likely to be overlooked or not speak up.

Compelling communication is about building presence – specifically leadership presence. For me, this is an energy of authority, credibility and assuredness within ourselves. With this comes authenticity and trust. Without compelling communication we blend in, we're more likely to be overlooked, and perceived to be lacking confidence and competence. If you don't sound confident, why would anyone believe what you're saying? Why would anyone follow you or choose to work with you?

*Only through communication can human life hold meaning.*

~ Paulo Freire

Qualifying phrases communicate we're unsure. These are used at the beginning of the sentence and function as a 'get out of jail free' card. For example, statements such as: 'Well, I could be wrong, but ... ', or 'I don't have much experience in this area ...', or 'You know better than me about this'. There are times when the use of these are warranted, but if they become a default speech pattern, it reflects we're unsure.

Another speech habit is using an undermining structure. An example of this can be demonstrated when asking a question. Typically, we ask a question when we don't know the answer. When we ask a question, we use an upward tonality at the end of our sentence. By using the same speech structure to make a statement sound like a question, we're deflecting possible criticism.

Compare the following two statements:

*'Do you think we need to revisit our social media strategy?'*

*'I believe we need to revisit our social media strategy.'*

The first comment sounds like an uncertain suggestion. The second, conveys more certainty, as it's a statement, rather than a question. The message is the same but the effect is different.

Another undermining speech structure is speaking without punctuation – in an incessant stream. This is like the proverbial runaway train. Have you ever met someone that talks and talks without coming up for air? If you've experienced this, it can be frustrating, especially if you in believe in waiting for the speaker to finish before adding to the conversation. There's no space to digest or process what they've said and no space to respond without cutting them off.

The final undermining speech habit is what I call overemphasis with the word 'actually'. Such as, 'Actually, I have a question'. The word 'actually', creates additional emphasis and conveys surprise. Let's use the same sentence without overemphasis: 'I have a question'. The second version communicates certainty and is more powerful than the original. Are you someone who overemphasises or do you know others who have this pattern?

How do we use more compelling communication? Making a statement as a statement (without the upward inflection), is great first step. If you have a tendency to make sentences sound like questions, then changing this one habit will make a significant difference to the effectiveness of your communication.

The second step is to stop apologising. This is a common habit among women and something I feel very strongly about. So many women over-apologise and say they're sorry when they're not. I believe apologies have a place and are appropriate for when we're concerned or experiencing guilt or regret. Save apologising for when you're genuinely sorry. For example, when someone says, 'Sorry, I just have a question'. There's no need to apologise before asking a question!

Did you notice the double-whammy of undermining speech in the previous sentence with the words 'Sorry' and 'just' in the one statement! Why do women do this? I don't have a definitive answer, but I believe it's connected to wanting to be liked, wanting to be accepted and wanting to be right. We each have value to add with our questions, thinking and our perspective, so *own your value!*

Habits can only be changed if we have awareness and decide we want to change them. Together, we can empower our language and shift gender dynamics one conversation at a time. When you hear undermining language by another woman, find a way to let her know there's no need for an apology. Have the courage to share what you've learned with her in private, because she could be you.

Another way to deliver more compelling communication is to drop the use of minimisers – the use of 'just', and 'a bit' and 'a little'. The best use of these words is to defuse emotion and create space when conversation is becoming intense. The occasional 'just' or 'a bit' now and then is fine. It's excessive use of these that puts your credibility at risk.

Most people care about what others think of them. However, when our concern undermines the way we behave, we're not being ourselves. People pleasing and being what we think others want us to be is a recipe for exhaustion. We cannot take responsibility for how other people respond to us, and I believe, as women, it's time to step up our communication by owning our value and communicating this with conviction.

Mastering compelling communication involves knowing what to exclude as much as what to include. Bombarding people with information can suggest that you're not really sure what's needed or what's necessary, so you're throwing in everything. Knowing what to exclude is a quality shown by effective leaders, particularly in the information age. The tendency to over-communicate in emails and conversation reflects more about the sender or speaker wanting to showcase their knowledge, or being unclear about what's required, rather than their awareness of their audience.

Concise equals confidence. Concise is also more challenging to do well. The art of reducing your message takes a lot more skill than broadcasting everything you know or that comes to mind. A tip I've found useful is when writing concise emails, is to write the desired outcome as the first line on the email. That way, I'm able to refer back to this when I'm typing. If you try this technique, make sure you delete the line before hitting send! In the words of author and speaker, Simon Sinek, start with the end in mind.

## Chapter Five Practice

To deliver compelling communication, make the following a regular practice:

- **Get clear.** Record a meeting or conversation where you're participating. Listen back to the recording and notice any undermining speech habits or structure used by you or others. Often, we're not consciously aware of these patterns.
- **Get confident.** Save apologising for when you're genuinely sorry and develop two new default responses you can use instead. This could be, 'I made a mistake', or 'I seem to have stuffed

up'. To add to these, come up with a response for accidently bumping into someone.
- **Get leverage.** Drop your tonality at the end of sentences during meetings and save upward inflection for questions.
- **Get perspective.** When you hear undermining language habits by another woman, have the courage to share what you've learned with her in private.

## Your Chapter Five Commitments:

What is one thing from this chapter you are committing to taking action on now?

(space for writing)

_____
_____
_____
_____
_____
_____

# 6
# Unspoken Edge

*Your body communicates as well as your mouth. Don't contradict yourself.*

~ Allen Ruddock

Unspoken edge comes from our non-verbal communication via gestures and body language. They can be intentional and obvious or subtle. They can also be subconscious such as micro expressions. Some micro expressions we don't have much influence over, (like the dilation of our eye pupils).

Have you ever seen a TV commercial, movie, or a live concert where the character or performer was lip-synching and the audio didn't match up directly with what you're seeing? I'm sure you'll agree it's off-putting. There's something about the communication that doesn't just feel right. One of the ways that we build credibility is through trust. Trust is built through consistency, congruency and authenticity.

With lip-syncing, when what we see and hear aren't in sync, we notice and we lose trust. We prioritise what we see as stronger proof compared to what we hear, and this is why micro expressions are so important. Ever had a conversation and afterwards felt something wasn't quite right but couldn't specifically articulate why? A possibility is there was a mismatch of micro expressions compared with the other person's language.

Non-verbal communication is powerful. Our body language communicates emotion and adds depth to our message. It's a magnifier of our messages. People don't remember what you say as much as how you make them feel. We remember emotion more than content. Where there's a mismatch between words and actions, actions will prevail as the stronger message.

The technique actors use to create congruence with dialogue, body language and micro expressions is to go into the same emotional state as the character they're portraying. If the character is feeling sad and defeated, they will slump their shoulders forward, eyes will be cast down, and chin will be tilted downward. Taking this to the next level, is to immerse in the thinking of the character. How would the character be thinking at the time, what might they be saying to themselves and how would they be feeling? Great actors will go to that level of detail and deliver a compelling portrayal of a character.

When we change the way we move, the way we breathe and the way we hold ourselves, (our non-verbal communication) we change our body's chemistry. In her infamous TED talk, researcher Amy Cuddy shares her research on body language. During her presentation, she discusses how a simple power pose (e.g., Superman pose – standing tall with feet shoulder-width apart, hands on hips), has been shown to increase testosterone by 20% when held for two minutes. Testosterone is connected with decision making, doing and taking action. It reduces our cortisol (the stress hormone) by 18%.

Confident and congruent communication means our gestures need to match what we're saying, and our tonality also needs to match our intention. Most people have had a shopping experience where the sales assistant was doing everything right in terms of what they were saying, but their attitude and body language gave a completely different message. A traditional greeting such as, 'Hello, how are you today?', can create an experience of delight or despair for a customer.

*The most important thing in communication is hearing what isn't said.*

*~ Peter Drucker*

I had a recent experience at a supermarket checkout, where the cashier asked me how I was in a flat tone with no eye contact. I felt like I was speaking with a robot who was repeating a standard script and that my presence was an annoyance rather than welcomed. The cashier's non-verbal signals suggested they didn't want to be there and didn't wish to engage with customers at that moment.

How do we go about developing our unspoken edge? The first step is great posture. Standing tall, shoulders down, back and chest forward. Great posture communicates confidence, certainty, trustworthiness and an attitude of, 'I've got this'. In my opinion, it's by far, the sexiest accessory a woman can have! There is no excuse for having poor posture. An assessment by an osteopath, chiropractor, physiotherapist or personal trainer will give you specific feedback on how your posture is tracking and what you can do to achieve, correct or maintain great posture.

It's not uncommon to see women with shoulders rounded forwards in a subtle or slightly more pronounced hunch. Rounded-shoulders make you look less confident than having your shoulders down and back. This doesn't mean we should all walk around as if we're balancing a book on our head. Instead, build awareness of your posture and what it's communicating to those around you. I demonstrate this in my 'Own The Room' masterclass, and participants are surprised at how much difference a slight rounding of the shoulders makes to how confident they appear.

Bad posture can easily be reversed by strengthening (tightening) the upper back muscles and stretching (lengthening) the chest muscles. Building strong core muscles and engaging abdominal muscles is also important, because they support the lower back. Since my days as a personal trainer, gym supervisor and group fitness instructor, I've been a long-time advocate of strength training for women. It's an effective way to develop both physical and mental strength and only two sessions of strength-based training per week can deliver transformational results.

I'm very grateful for doing ballet, gymnastics and other physical activities in my early years, as they've contributed to a foundation of good posture. I remember attending ballet classes at Gay Whitman's Studio in North Balwyn. In one class, we were told to imagine we were puppets with a piece of string attached to the top of our head. We had to pretend the puppet master was slowly pulling the string up, making us stretch up and stand taller. While this was happening, the teacher walked around the class with her long cane and gently tapped any area that was not stretched or appropriately placed. We then had to maintain this upright posture for the entire class while we were doing our plie and arm exercises at the barre. At the time, I found this to be tedious, but now I value the contribution it's made towards my posture!

Fast forward a few years to secondary school. I sang in the school choir for about three years. This meant many rehearsal hours spent standing up straight while we were singing. My music teacher, Miss Beckett, had a cheeky sense of humour. At each rehearsal we were reminded to improve our posture as it effected the quality of our voices and the overall sound of the choir. Each practice and each performance, Miss Beckett would repeat the same two-word instruction: 'Boobies up!' just before we began singing – it got our attention! This was to became an anchor and it worked well with a group of school-aged girls.

The reason I have focused on posture is because it's important if you want to put your most confident self forward. Here are the essentials for great a posture: the first step is to get fitted with a proper bra by a professional fitter. If you're uncomfortable standing with your shoulders back and down, it may be because you're wearing a bra that doesn't fit well. A great fitting bra can make a world of difference to self-confidence for some women. So, if you've had some self-confidence issues around your bust line, whether you feel too big or too small, get fitted with a great bra.

The next step to great posture is practice and self-awareness. What's your posture like when you're sitting down and standing up? Some women have a tendency to sit with their shoulders rounded forward and their bottom sitting forward in the chair – making themselves physically smaller. Sometimes women perch on the front edge of the seat. It's a pattern I see frequently. Self-awareness is key. Sitting up straight in the chair, with your bottom in the back of the seat is a simple, yet very effective way to create instant presence and energy. You'll feel more engaged when you're sitting up straight and more switched on.

Another powerful use of non-verbal communication is eye contact. A powerful way to connect is by holding someone's gaze – and I don't mean having a staring competition! Hold eye contact when meeting someone for the first time, rather than looking away too quickly. Shifting eyes that dart around, make a person look nervous and unconfident. The aim is to maintain enough eye contact long enough so that you feel connected.

Think about going to an event for the very first time where you don't know anyone. For some people, it's not a big deal. For others, they may feel uncomfortable and quite nervous. If you do feel uncomfortable and nervous, think about how you're holding your whole body. What's your posture like? How are you holding your shoulders? Are your eyes looking at eye level or cast slightly down? When you make eye contact, do you quickly look away or maintain the gaze for a moment? What are your hands doing, are they fidgeting? There are many components to non-verbal communication. My suggestion is to focus on one area at a time. If there's an area that comes immediately to mind for improvement, start with this and keep your practice focused on this until you feel competent.

A must-have accessory for your unspoken edge is a firm handshake. A firm handshake is not one that's bone crushing! A firm handshake is steady, feels secure and lasts for approximately one to two seconds. A firm handshake conveys confidence and certainty.

During one of my Own the Room masterclasses, the group was discussing their impressions of someone with a firm handshake compared to someone with a soft or limp, handshake. Responses to a limp handshake included: a feeling of distrust towards the person, a perception they're cold or standoffish, they appeared superficial, seemed like a push-over and seemed nervous. All this from a handshake!

In contrast, feedback from a firm handshake, included: the person is confident, they're firm but fair, this person is dependable, reliable, credible, they're a good leader, they're in control and they know what they want. A firm handshake conveys confidence and credibility. Next time you're shaking someone's hand, repeat these three simple yet powerful words (internally) to reinforce a physical state of confidence: 'I've got this'.

Sometimes I'm asked, 'If I'm in a long meeting, how do I hold an upright posture for a lengthy period of time?'. My suggestion is to make sitting up straight your normal way of sitting. This might take some adjustment, depending on your fitness or any specific back issues. Get some guidance on how to build the muscle group that supports your lower back – your core muscles. A strong core means a strong back.

In order to stand up straight without feeling like a soldier, keep your shoulders down and back, your chest up, and remember to move your arms – otherwise you'll look like you're standing to attention! I invite you and encourage you to seek out a communication buddy, someone who you can partner with for feedback. This is a way to fast track your progress.

Stand big. Standing big means standing with your arms beside your body – not with your hands clasped in front of you. If that feels unnatural, have something in one hand, so one arm can be bent at a ninety-degree angle (e.g., a glass in your hand, or a pen or a clicker if you're presenting slides). One arm beside your body and one at a right angle is an easy position to maintain and gives you a look of openness and credibility.

## Chapter Six Practice

To develop powerful physicality, make the following a regular practice:

- **Get clear. Have your posture assessed by your health practitioner of choice (osteo, physio, chiro or personal trainer). Commit to corrective activity where appropriate.**
- **Get confident. Get professionally fitted for a bra.**
- **Get leverage. Sit taller during meetings and notice the shift in room dynamics.**
- **Get perspective. Before an important call or presentation, stand in your superhero pose and repeat to yourself, 'I've got this'.**

## Your Chapter Six Commitments:

What is one thing from this chapter you are committing to taking action on now?

(space for writing)

_____
_____
_____
_____
_____
_____
_____
_____
_____
_____
_____

# 7
## Congruent Currency

*A bird doesn't sing because it has an answer, it sings because it has a song.*

~ Maya Angelou

Your 10 X value is your personal currency – how we utilise our personal power and package our personal currency. This is when you're at your most valuable and compelling, because how you do what you do, is what stands you apart.

The closest we come to defining who we are is when we're clear about our core values. We may have conscious awareness of what they are, or we may not. Our core values are what we believe to be important, what we uphold to be our truth, make decisions by and live our lives in accordance with.

Who we are is our personal currency and our personal power base. Some women don't feel like they know who they really are or what they do well. In a world where independent contractors and small business are becoming more prevalent, it's time to get clear on the value you bring and connect with your personal currency. With this, we're able to infuse more of our unique talents and personality into our roles, our businesses and how we do what we do.

Our personal currency is also our source of influence and where we demonstrate leadership naturally. Martin Luther King Junior describes power as the ability to effect change. I believe personal currency is our greatest asset and leverage within the context of having the most potential to influence.

Power is not about command and conquer, although it can be interpreted this way. Our beliefs about our talent, skills and values *will* influence and *do* influence our decision making, behaviour and our pro-activeness to be more visible.

We're unique; there is no one else the same as us. Even identical twins will still have their own individual talents and qualities. Their thinking is different and their ability to perform tasks is different. They share a lot of things in common, but they are not the same person. The great news about being unique, is that no one has an identical perspective or shares the same thinking as you. What you offer and have the ability to contribute is uniquely yours!

Our thumbprint is our imprint. What makes us different, even in subtle ways, is how we create contrast. When we combine this with what we care about, we're adding emotion to what we do. Call it energy, enthusiasm, dedication or passion – if we feel what we're doing is related to something worthwhile, we're more engaged in our work, more engaging to be around and more likely to communicate with impact.

## COMMUNICATION IMPACT

| Emotion | | | |
|---|---|---|---|
| | Moving | Compelling | Captivating |
| | Engaging | Interesting | Intriguing |
| | Invisible | Emerging | Challenging |

Contrast

Emphasising your differences makes you memorable, but people are moved more by your emotion for what you do. If you're the same as the majority and have little passion for what you do, it's a recipe for staying invisible. You can move people with your passion, even if what you do is the same as what many others do.

Embracing and valuing your individual mix of history and experiences, perspective, thinking and skills, is powerful when used for marketing and positioning in your business, or promoting yourself to be considered for other roles or passion projects. Whether you're a business owner or working in an organisation, articulating your unique strengths makes you more promotable. A client of mine summed this up beautifully when she said, 'Now that I know what my core values are, what I stand for and my unique strengths, I have clarity around my messaging. When people ask me what I do, I feel more confident answering and after I tell them, they want to know more. My marketing messages are much easier to communicate too.'

Accurate statistics for small business survival rates are limited. In a summary by the Small Business Development Corporation in Western Australia, between June 2011 and June 2015, 42% of non-employing businesses, were still operating after four years, and for businesses employing 1-19 people, the figure was 52% (based on ABS business count data). Acknowledging the higher rates of mining and construction related businesses in Western Australia, this data is still comparable with figures by other sources. The point here is, many small businesses are not operating after four years and there are many factors contributing to this.

Excluding reasons of mergers, take-overs, name changes, industry changes and retirement. I believe one of the biggest contributing factors to business survival rates, particularly for professional services, is invisible or ineffective marketing. This is where the business owner is unable to articulate what they stand for, who they are or why a prospective customer should do business with them. When we don't infuse our personal currency into the work we do, we become transactional and seen as a commodity. So, if a business has quirky as a core value, how is this applied across all customer touch points, from their website to their hold music?

Many skills are transferable and in the future, some jobs and roles will become obsolete and new ones will be invented. Professional growth is about transferable skills. For example, if you're naturally wired to notice detail, you will notice detail in whatever role you're in. For example, a barrister, will do well through astute observation of facts and detail that may change the outcome of a court case. Accordingly, a barista who notices detail will most likely make great coffee consistently! They'll pay close attention to details such as how the coffee beans are roasted, the temperature of the milk, the foam stability, pouring technique and so on.

Some roles are skill specific. If you're wanting to be a reconstructive surgeon, there is a formal path of recognised learning and training in specific skills needed. Yet, two highly skilled surgeons, can still offer a different experience, dependent on their communication style, their training, their innate sense of proportion and visual aesthetics and personality.

Generic personal and business brands that promote a person's job or career position (such as a tax accountant), are more likely to be seen as transactional businesses. These businesses attract customers who just want a specific service or who need to get 'the job done' and generally for the cheapest price. These types of client are more likely to make their decision based on, 'What can I get for the least amount of money?'. With this thinking, they are also more likely to expect the result to be equivalent of a premium priced competitor and will complain when it's not.

Have you heard the expression, 'We can't see the picture when we're in the frame'? This is when we don't see or experience ourselves the same way others do. If we've had to overcome challenges to become good at something, we're likely to be more effective teachers, compared with someone who is a naturally talented at this. The perspective and empathy we've developed along the way are valuable resources we can use to teach others.

In Year 11, I had physics teacher who was a brilliant man. He was quietly spoken with a gentle disposition and everyone liked him. He knew the curriculum well (because he wrote the text book used by schools!), yet regularly students could not understand the principals he was trying to teach. It was second nature to him and gobbled-gook to us.

Feedback is a wonderful thing, although I didn't always share this view. Years ago, if I had received negative feedback, I would internalise it, dwell on it and try to overcompensate. Growing up, I had a hang up about my fair skin, which was really a reflection of low self-esteem. Nowadays, I regularly receive positive feedback on my grooming and how I present myself. This is an example of a learned skill I developed growing up, after regular feedback about looking washed-out, or looking scruffy. Without conscious awareness I have become attuned to which colours suit my skin tone, what clothing styles suit my body, what proportions work and what don't. Ultimately (and without awareness), I became good at presenting myself because I wanted to avoid criticism about my appearance.

Let's say you're a speaker in the area of leadership – that's your niche. So far, you're grouped with other leadership speakers. To create a point of difference, let's add your speciality and apply this to your niche. The best way to go about specialising, is choosing an area which includes your personal currency. For example, if you're naturally witty and humorous, your speeches and presentations will most likely have a humorous flavour to them. If you're very good at facts, research and love statistics, your delivery is more likely to be well-researched with up to the minute facts, compelling case studies and trends. Compare these two examples with a leadership speaker who is futuristic-focussed and digs technology. Their style of delivery might be an exploration about the future of leadership and where leadership is headed. They may also use some new gadgets or technology as part of their presentation.

Using the above example of three speakers with a niche in leadership, whilst they may speak about the same topic area, they represent a different value proposition for a speaking engagement. Each speaker brings her personal currency to differentiate her delivery and audience experience. Using your personal currency means you're able to market yourself more specifically, be referred more easily and create alliances with those whom you may have previously considered competition. It also means you'll be invited to do engagements that are more suited to what you do best, allowing you to deliver at your best.

How do we get clear on our personal currency? There are many ways to approach this. I've chosen three effective ways to do just that. The first one utilises one of the profiling tools I have mentioned previously – specifically, the How to Fascinate™ profile. Online there is a free mini version (and you'll be asked if you want to upgrade to learn more about you!). What I love about this profiling tool, is it explores how the world sees us. Not in the context of seeking external validation, but from the perspective of our unique strengths and when we're at our most valuable. We are not always aware of how we are perceived by others. As the saying goes, 'We can't read the label when we're in the jar'.

Sometimes your personal currency is not what you think it is. Quite often, it's not the job title you have now. There will be something about how you do what you do that makes you valuable and positions you to become your most remarkable self. How will you know? You will feel a conviction that what you're doing matters, you'll want to keep doing it and you'll be doing it well.

*The thing that seems so easy to you is your talent, your gift. You're certain anyone could do it but they can't.*

~ Unknown

The second way to identify your personal currency is to invite and seek feedback. I think feedback has been misinterpreted as criticism. It's easy to view feedback as something we subject ourselves to as part of quality assurance metrics or because its compulsory for our role. Being okay with feedback is being open to other people communicating how you can connect with them better.

Ironically, feedback is often more about the person giving the feedback than the person it's directed at. If you've just spoken at a group meeting and someone in the audience says you need to slow down, there may be some truth in that. What they're really telling you is: for them to connect with your messages, they need more time to think through what you've said. You will notice trends and themes in the feedback you receive (which will evolve over time). It's also worth noting the source of feedback to acknowledge what perspective they may be coming from and help you assess the validity of the feedback.

Feedback is a platform for personal growth. Proactively seeking feedback from others is a valuable way to build self-awareness. A philosophy I learned during my coach training is, 'The person with the most self-awareness wins'. This means that the person with the most self-awareness has the most behavioural flexibility and is most adaptable in any given situation.

The third way of increasing your personal currency is selecting a platform mode that's a match for you. I believe we have a preference of working with one of the following four:

- **people**
- **systems**
- **things**
- **concepts**

Circle the one you feel most relates to you. Are you drawn more to people interaction, face-to-face communication and connection? Or perhaps you prefer systems, making sure activities flow smoothly? What about things – do you enjoy making and creating tangible items? Perhaps concepts and ideas are more your style? Or do you like to work with ideas and strategy? Being clear on your preferred platform mode helps set you up to be your remarkable self and do your best work.

The next step is to select your preferred communication mode. Look at the list below and select your top two (feel free to add to the list also):

- **speaking**
- **writing**

- singing
- demonstrating
- building
- creating
- acting
- translating
- solving
- inventing

What's your preferred way of communicating your message and sharing your talents? Now that you've selected your preferred platform and communication mode, brainstorm on a piece of paper how these might work synergistically. For example, if you prefer dealing with things and you love to talk, then a good match for you could be to share your message with a podcast series. When you combine your platform with your preferred communication modes, you're setting yourself up to communicate in ways that highlight your talents.

Build greater insights into your desirable qualities with what I call the Three Words Activity. The Three Words Activity is where you send out an e-mail to people you know (ranging from very well to acquaintance), asking them which three words best describe your most desirable attributes? If you're feeling game, you may also ask for the three words to describe your least desirable attributes. I strongly invite you to do this activity. At the end of it, you'll see themes and patterns that are very informative – it's really worth doing.

Complete the How to Fascinate™ profile and/or complete the Strengths Finder 2.0™. Both are very insightful, low cost tools to guide you towards your personal currency so you can bring your best to what you do and become even more valuable.

You can find these at www.howtofascinate.com and www.strengthstest.com.

## Chapter Seven Practice

To grow your unique talent, make the following a regular practice:

- **Get clear.** Complete as many profiling tools as possible.
- **Get confident.** Identify your personal currency with the Three Word Activity.
- **Get leverage.** Use your personal currency in your marketing copy and messages.
- **Get perspective.** What is your preferred mode? Choose one and commit to creating content via this channel. If it doesn't seem a match, choose a different one.

## Your Chapter Seven Commitments:

What is one thing from this chapter you are committing to taking action on now?

(space for writing)

_____

_____

_____

_____

_____

_____

_____

_____

_____

_____

_____

# 8
# Re-Wire

*Our bodies change our minds, and our minds change our behaviour, and our behaviour changes our outcomes.*

~ Amy Cuddy

Finding space in our busy lives is a daily challenge for many. Re-wire is about finding space, letting go of exhaustion as a status symbol, and letting go of busyness as a metric for self-worth. We live in a culture which prizes busyness over meaningful contribution. Shifting our thinking from the busyness of now and creating space to recharge and reconnect with ourselves gives us better emotional control.

With better emotional control, we are better parents, partners, colleagues, friends, and daughters. With better emotional control, our thinking is clearer, we feel physically calmer and we sleep better. Cognitively, we perform better and have more energy. It's about bringing our best selves to each day, both physically and mentally and creating more desirable biochemistry to boot!

Health is our most valuable asset. Without our health, not much else matters. As a nation, we're experiencing obesity, overmedication and anxiety at alarming levels. When we don't look after ourselves we feel exhausted and grumpy and make poor decisions. This takes a toll on relationships, families and detracts from our quality of life.

Making space in our lives for creativity, ideas and problem solving is valuable for generating perspective. I believe we all share the same purpose – to be the best version of us, so we can contribute in our own unique way. I prefer an inclusive definition of purpose which opens up possibilities, as well as creating freedom to follow different missions and passions in our lives.

Over time, we will explore different missions based on our thinking at the time, shifting peripheral values and life circumstances. Having mental space to connect with what we care about, allows our mind to problem solve organically and explore future possibilities for achieving our next level.

I remember early on in my business, feeling up to my eyeballs in work, feeling like I still had so much more to do and working overtime without much to show for it. I couldn't see how to move past what I felt was a huge road block. So I arranged an appointment with a mentor. I prepared for the session, put together a summary of my goals, current status with these, the activities I was doing and what I wanted to achieve from our session together.

Early into the session, this mentor suggested I needed to create some white space. 'White space?' I asked. 'What do you mean white space?' She explained to me that I needed to block out time to get some perspective. I was annoyed … Didn't she get what I was telling her? Didn't she understand that my challenge was how can I do more when I'm already maxed out? No, she understood, better than I did. With the amount of activity I was doing, I had lost my ability to see the big picture and to prioritise. I was too busy 'doing' and saying yes to everything, rather than focusing my energies on what mattered most.

The following week after this session, I became run down with a nasty cold. I wondered how I was going get through my To Do list – I didn't and it was a blessing in disguise. The situation forced me to decide what to prioritise and what to let go of. Added to this was the benefits of having to rest up. It was during this time I experienced a clarity about my priorities that I had not experienced for a while.

Re-Wire is about respecting ourselves through respecting our health. Imagine approaching self-care with the same level of professionalism we bring to our careers and work life. How different would your health be? It's been said that the most important measure of success are the friends we have and the quality of the relationships we have. That has nothing to do with exhaustion or business and everything to do with quality of life. How do we Re-Wire and create more space in our lives? Firstly, we need to make moments for quiet reflection to recharge our mind, body and spirit.

Sleep is something that a quick straw poll shows most of us feel we don't consistently get enough of, or lack quality of. We're intelligent, we know sleep is important. A lack of sleep produces greater amounts of stress related hormones and an anxious brain. Under these conditions, we're not bringing our best game to what we do.

The average adult needs seven and a half to eight hours sleep a night. Professor Richard Wiseman, a psychologist at the University of Hertfordshire, commissioned a YouGov poll to assess the sleep habits of adults. Of the 2,149 adults surveyed, 59% reported sleeping for seven hours or less a night – an increase from 39% polled the year before.

Professor Wiseman also reported that the blue light emitted by our electronic devices, surpasses the production of sleep inducing hormone, melatonin, reducing drowsiness and making it harder to fall asleep. Professor Wiseman recommends avoiding these devices two hours before bedtime. That's all electronic devices, including your phone, television and iPad/tablet. Even if you still fall asleep after looking at a screen up until bedtime, it will take you longer to fall asleep and your sleep quality won't be as good. Our brain needs time to wind down from focussed work, so if you're up late sending work emails, your mind has not switched off when you go to bed. It will still be processing work-related thoughts, rather than being in a state of physical and mental relaxation.

Movement is another vital component to Re-Wire. I believe exercise is an investment and a privilege. After working in some of Melbourne's largest hospitals as a dietitian, I saw many previously well women in their 60s, 70s, and 80s admitted to the orthopaedics ward after having a fall and sustaining a broken femur (hip bone). Frequently, their quality of life deteriorated severely after this from losing muscle tone and strength during their stay. They'd also suffer weight loss, but above all, they'd lose their confidence. During rehabilitation, they would take the steps, but rarely regain the confidence they had prior to their fall. It was not uncommon for them to be readmitted the following year from another fall.

According to Australian Bureau of Statistics, 63.4% of Australians, are overweight or obese – that's around 11.2 million people! Rates in Australia show the biggest increase in a survey of almost 200 countries, making us one of the fattest nations in the world. This is not an achievement to be proud of. It's a reflection of a lifestyle of energy imbalance. We have a variety of labour-saving devices so we don't have to move nearly as much as we did. I urge you to get up out of your seat regularly and move. Do it now! It makes a difference and you matter.

*Take care of your body, it's the only place you have to live.*
~ Jim Rohn

One of the philosophies I subscribe to is taking the stairs wherever possible. Unless I'm carrying something particularly heavy or large, taking the stairs is my default behaviour. Shift your mindset so stairs (or your nominated activity) become what you *expect* to do, rather than what you *have to do*. This will become a new normal for you, and you'll experience the positive results that come with that.

Many years ago, I worked in a Country Road store. It was approaching Christmas time and in the first two weeks I lost a few kilos without aiming to. I still ate the same. Nothing else had changed other than working in the store. It was a large store and it was busy. It had a stock room, tea room and toilets located up several flights of stairs. This meant I was climbing hundreds of stairs each day and doing considerably more walking than I had been doing prior to working there. It was a reminder that moving constantly (and taking the stairs!) uses more energy than sitting down for most of the day. If you're experiencing a gradual accumulation of weight each year, this may be relevant. We're living longer, so if we want our body to go the distance and want to experience a better quality of life, we need to move it and challenge it.

I find strength training empowering, and the women I've worked with and groups I've trained share similar feedback. The comments that come back are: I feel empowered, I feel strong, I feel more confident. Each strength training activity becomes an opportunity to create mini defining moments and achievements. It's a great way to train both mind and body. Each time you're having to push through physical discomfort, you're backing yourself in that moment. It becomes cyclical; the more you back yourself, the more accustomed you become to backing yourself. Just do that!

The other obvious benefit of strength training is in maintaining an appropriate weight. Regular strength training conditions your muscles to burn more fuel twenty-four hours a day, which is really beneficial for maintaining weight. Being an appropriate weight comes with having more energy. So if you're feeling tired or exhausted, when is now a good time to make a change and have more energy?

One thing I learned many years ago during my work in the fitness industry, is that we lose an average of 5% of our muscle mass every ten years after the age of thirty-five. This means it's easier to slowly gain weight after this age. Strength training activities are important, as they use calories during and after workouts – if you train with enough intensity. Also keep in mind, if you're wanting to lose weight, do add in some kind of resistance exercise, otherwise a lot of the weight you lose will come from muscle as well as fat. As the saying goes, 'use it or lose it'. Our muscle mass contributes to maintaining our metabolic rate – the rate at which we burn calories and achieve energy balance.

You can appreciate how rituals such as the introduction of wine each night, a chai latte each day or a biscuit from the jar at work with each coffee will add up. These rituals effect our overall energy balance and may contribute to gaining weight without trying – also known as *calorie creep*! Turning this around is easy: add resistance training into your week. Find the best way to make it work for you: joining group training, working with a personal trainer, getting an accountability buddy, or going solo and listening to your favourite music or podcast while you're working out.

A calmer mind is the result of Re-Wire. Meditation is the ultimate tool for a calmer and more confident mind. Meditation is a practice of mind relaxation using continued or extended thought, reflection or contemplation. Meditation can be guided or self-guided, using verbal mantras and chants or in silence. It can be done while sitting up or lying down. It's not the type of mediation that counts, it's the consistency.

Areas where evidence supports the benefits of meditation include: better mental focus, improved memory, better stress management, improved emotional resilience, better decision making, lower blood pressure, improvements in immune system function, weight management, pain management and even improved relationships.

In the *Journal of the American Medical Association, Internal Medicine,* Dr Madhav Goyal and colleagues report mindfulness meditation showing moderate benefits for improving anxiety, depression and pain. Meditation is an accessible way for everyone to feel better!

The fear centre within the brain, known as the amygdala, responds through a form of atrophy to meditation, and shrinks in size. A study using MRI imaging with self-proclaimed stressed executives showed they were able to change their negative, habitual thought patterns after using self-guided meditation over an eight-week period, for five to ten minutes a day.

There are many different forms of meditation, which means there is something for everyone! You may find using chanting to create a resonate sound to be an effective form of meditation. Alternatively, focusing on an image or colour may be your preference. My personal choice is to allow the mind space to be open and to explore whatever's coming through my mind in a detached way, like an outside observer. I believe building space into our lives for meditation creates a space for our mind to explore whatever is challenging us in a non-judgemental way.

Some people say, 'I don't have time to meditate' or 'You don't get how busy I am'. I appreciate the busyness of life. The great thing about meditation is it can be done within minutes. Watch one less hour of television each day (or none at all!) and there's a week's worth of meditation time.

There is no definitive study on the minimum length of time needed to meditate for ultimate benefits. What is known and what's agreed upon is consistency. To begin with, give yourself a goal of five minutes. Set the clock timer on your phone, and sit somewhere quiet, away from distractions and allow your thoughts to move through your mind. See what comes up without attachment or judgement. You can even do this in the car after you pull into your driveway or just before walking into the office in the morning. There is no specific time to meditate either. You can do this first thing in the morning, last thing at night or perhaps in the shower!

You'll know the best way to find those five minutes. If that seems like a stretch, go with sixty seconds. I don't believe anyone who says they can't find sixty seconds to do this. It's a simple and rewarding habit. I invite you to set yourself a meditation goal. Choose the goal that's suitable for you – sixty seconds, five minutes, or forty-five minutes! Make the goal small and realistic so you feel a sense of accomplishment that'll encourage you to keep going.

I don't prescribe a set amount of time when it comes to sleeping. I believe we each know through trial and error over the years, how much sleep we feel we need to operate at our best. How are you choosing to spend your evenings – watching television, working on your laptop, reading a book or engaging in a hobby? How might you rearrange your evening activities to give your mind quiet time to rest?

I recommend a digital detox. A report by the Radicati Group, estimates the average person receives 121 business-related emails a day. This is expecting to increase to 140 by 2018! I was astounded when I read this! Is this you? Try a digital detox, for one day and see what difference that makes in your life.

Explore strength training and think about how you can incorporate this into the activity that you do. After experiencing different styles of strength training, my personal favourite is high intensity interval training twice a week. I find this helps me maintain a level of strength and lean body mass. Give it a go, experiment with different forms of strength training and see what works for you. In a recent class I attended, the instructor said to the group, 'fitness is not physical, it's all mental'. I agree with this; our bodies are capable of more than we realise. Much of the challenge we face with fitness is persisting even when we don't feel like it.

## Chapter Eight Practice

To improve your energy, make the following a regular practice:

- **Get clear. Set a meditation goal: length of time, place and preferred approach. Start now.**
- **Get confident. Experiment with and incorporate strength training into your week.**
- **Get leverage. Boost your sleep quality with a screen-free hour before bedtime.**
- **Get perspective. Set your challenge and give yourself a digital detox. This could be for one hour, one evening or one day.**

## Your Chapter Eight Commitments:

What is one thing from this chapter you are committing to taking action on now?

(space for writing)

_____

_____

_____

_____

_____

_____

_____

_____

_____

_____

# PART THREE

# PROSPERITY

# 9
# New You

*One's mind, once stretched by a new idea, never regains its original dimensions.*

~ Oliver Wendell Holmes

The new you has a clear direction and the ability to prioritise. The new you is well practiced at saying no to things that aren't helping you achieve what matters to you. The new you makes decisions and choices, rather than saying yes to whatever opportunities come up. Some opportunities are valuable and some are fun – select those which take you in the direction you wish to go personally and/or professionally.

There are times for recreation and play and these are just as crucial as investing time to focus on growth. Prioritise what is most important. Doing these activities first thing each day, contributes to a feeling of meaningful accomplishment and structures our activities in a way that's congruent with our values. I'm a fan of having lists, and I confess to adding things to my list (even tasks I've already done) just to experience the satisfaction of crossing them off!

The new you is on a mission to conquer over-thinking and the need to please others. The new you recognises perfectionism is a reflection of low self-worth and holds people back from taking action – action that leads to further growth.

## RELATIONSHIP WITH SUCCESS

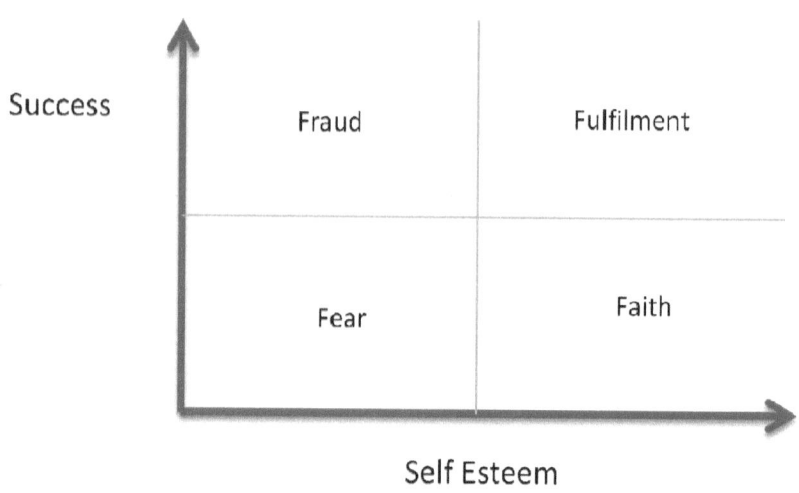

Our relationship with success and fulfilment is relative to our self-esteem. With a healthy self-esteem we experience fulfilment when we achieve success (however you choose to define success). In a Huffington Post article, Sheryl Sandberg, Maya Angelou and Tina Fey, have all publicly admitted to feeling like a fraud, despite their achievements. Without a robust self-esteem, there may be a sense of not deserving your accomplishments and success.

A robust self-esteem does not guarantee results. Women with robust self-esteem, do not automatically experience successful results. Instead, they operate from a place of faith in themselves, faith they will achieve and faith that an investment in training, mentoring or upskilling is worthwhile to help them become who they need to be– rather than what they need to be.

If self-esteem is low and success lacking (according to our individual definition of success), we might be experiencing life from a place of fear – fear of what others think, fear of being wrong, fear of not being enough and fear of not being liked. Our lack of results compounds this in a self-perpetuating cycle.

Moving closer to what we want to achieve is the difference between living proactively and living reactively. The aim is not to fill every hour of the day. With effective use of our time by prioritising what matters most, we free up space for family, friends, rest and play. What would you do with an extra hour per day? One solution could be to replace an hour of television with some much needed R & R (reading a book, having a bubble bath, calling a friend). Use this time to rediscover a hobby or connect with friends and family. Let these activities be the reward needed to prioritise what you choose to do each day.

Let's make the most of how our brain is wired. When we're told not to think of the pink elephant, typically the first thing we think of is the pink elephant. If we're buying a car and we've made a decision on what sort of car we want, we start noticing this type of car on the road. The cars were always there, yet we become even more aware when our focus is tuned into this type of car. That's our reticular activation system (RAS) in action.

Our RAS is a filter between our conscious thoughts and subconscious thoughts. The RAS is instrumental for achieving goals, because it's tuned into what we're focussed on. An article by Catherine Plano in online community blog, Flying Solo, claims setting goals works well with our RAS, because even when we're not consciously thinking about our goals, the brain knows they're important and makes a note of anything that's relevant to them.

If we're not connected to something meaningful, or don't feel like we're making a difference, we run the risk of turning to drama to meet our need for connection. It's an unhealthy relationship, but commonly used to feel important and worthy. I've seen this play out and perhaps you have too. Ever noticed people who seem to enjoy getting together and talking about what they hate, who did what, how horrible this or that was, and share the dramas of their lives? There's a pattern: someone will begin the conversation with their misfortune and another person will contribute their hard luck story and soon it becomes a spiral of who's got the worst life, until it becomes a big pity party! That's not to say dramas don't happen – life offers plenty of challenges to us all. I'm referring to people who seem to consistently talk about gossip and misfortune. Have you ever met someone who seems to always have drama in their life? Are you one of these people?

Most people have experienced loss, rejection and other unfortunate events in their life. When we choose to give ongoing energy and focus to those thoughts, we're building neural pathways in our brain, making it easier to default to negative thinking.

New you is about building self-awareness, deciding what matters most and moving beyond the fear of discomfort to experience fulfilment. What does success look like for you? How does that compare to where you are now? Identify which quadrant you feel best matches your relationship with success in the diagram. Why do you believe this is? What else is this about?

What difference do you want to make in the world? It's okay if you don't have a clear answer. I recommend you put aside fifteen minutes or more to reflect on this, and keep doing this over time at regular intervals, until you see similar ideas emerging. If you were to be known for one thing during your lifetime what do you want this to be? What is the recurring theme in your life, the consistent message or topic that connects the different things you've done? How have you been able to do the things you've done in a way that is uniquely you? If your signature is a word, what might that word be? To develop the new you, where are you choosing to focus your attention?

*It's not where you're going, it's how you get there.*

~ Unknown

Creating a results-driven mindset, shifts the focus from problem to solution. We want to limit problem-focussed thinking because if we dwell on the problem, it will build in magnitude, which creates feelings of stress and overwhelm.

What we perceive to be the problem is masking a deeper, underlying issue. The problem becomes a convenient distraction in avoiding confrontation. As long as we have what we believe to be a problem, we keep ourselves safe and avoid having to take action. For example, we complain about how we're super busy at work. If we fixate on this and the ramifications of this – 'If I go out on the weekend, I'll get behind with work. If I go on holiday, I'll get even further behind' – we create an effective distraction from the other challenges we might have (e.g., a dysfunctional relationship, dealing with unwell parents, improving our own health, etc.).

Choose who you spend time with and who you have conversations with wisely. When a friend is having a tough time, be there for them and create a space for them to vent. Make it clear to them you're here, and you want to help them move beyond their frustrations. You're next step is a new way of approaching what happens next. Here are five simple steps to help you and your friend get rid of frustration easily and effectively:

- **Allocate two minutes for your friend to vent. Set the timee on your phone.**
- **Invite your friend to give it their best, no holding back. They can yell, move around, even swear if it helps.**
- **If they run out of steam before the two minutes are up, encourage them to keep going. Get them to punch a cushion or pillow.**
- **When the two minutes are up, let them know their time is up, and be firm with this.**
- **Remind them any further conversations on this topic must be solutions-focussed only and ask for their commitment with this.**

It's a cathartic experience providing a safe space to vent frustrations in an animated way, as it helps release any intense emotions the person is feeling. At the end of this, there is generally a feeling of calm and even bouts of laughter on occasion. Once the intense emotions are released, your friend should be less reactive and have a clearer perspective moving forward.

It's not going to work in every situation. Sometimes there may be residual negative emotions. It is a highly effective way to deactivate brewing resentment or frustration and is preferable than your friend repeating the same problem over again. If they start to loop in their conversation, they may be meeting their need for connection through drama and they may not want to have their challenge solved.

Another way to approach developing a new you is to set a criteria for decision making. What we say no to is equally as important as what we say yes to. When we consistently put other people's priorities first, we're accepting they are more important than us and we're not as worthy.

Years ago I remember walking into someone's office, and reading a sign behind their desk at eye level that read: 'Your failure to plan, does not mean it's my problem'. This person would frequently assist with time-sensitive issues, but the point was clear – don't walk into my office at the last minute with your problem and expect me to drop everything because you haven't been organised.

The new you *cares about you*, and considers your priorities when making decisions. Effective decision making allows you to feel empowered to take action based on what you care about, rather than what others think you should care about. Ultimately, we find time for the things that matter most.

## Chapter Nine Practice

To grow into the new you, make the following a regular practice:

- **Get clear.** What does success look like specifically for you? Write it down in detail.
- **Get confident.** Shift your focus to what outcomes you want, not what you don't.
- **Get leverage.** Choose the people you spend time with carefully. Have a friend clean out if necessary. Yes, it's challenging, but **remember** *you've got this*!
- **Get perspective.** Use the five steps to venting for a friend or for you.

## Your Chapter Nine Commitments:

What is one thing from this chapter you are committing to taking action on now?

(space for writing)

_____
_____
_____
_____
_____
_____

# 10
## Authentic Influence

*15% of one's financial success is due to one's technical knowledge and 85% is due to skills in human engineering – leadership & influencing people.*

~ Dale Carnegie

In previous chapters, we looked at how authenticity refers to being aligned with our core values and what really matters to us. For example, if we value health, a rewarding role might be aligned with creating better health outcomes for others. With our work aligned to our core values, we bring passion to what we do – passion is a powerful form of influence that inspires action. How we communicate and commercialise our talents is the secret ingredient to ongoing authentic influence.

Authentic influence is about creating the outcomes we want, in the way we want and with the people we want. We need money to sustain our lifestyles, put food on the table and give us the freedom of choice. To achieve this, it's important to structure our business, so that access to us comes at a premium. Even being selective about the meetings we say yes to and additional projects we take on.

Everyone is in the business of sales and selling. It doesn't matter what your profession is, you're in the business of communicating to create influence of some sort. What people really buy is *you* – your values, how you live them and communicate them. You can create prosperity based on solving a problem you care about, and delivering this solution through your products, services or skills in a way that's valued by the market.

What specific problem do you solve? It's important to communicate the value of what we're offering beyond the product, service or skill. What sets us free is making the shift from a time-for-money, to a values-based business model. A great example of this came from a podcast I was listening to on the weekend. A woman was talking about her business, which specialises in streamlining payroll procedures and saving clients money – often millions. When she pitches her business to corporate clients, they ask what her day rate is so they can compare providers. She refuses to give a day rate. Logically, if you're able to save an organisation one million dollars and if the cost to them is $100K, is a daily rate relevant? This woman has a great track record and typically achieves great results for the client in a lot less time than her competition. The turning point for her in her business was when she switched from what she can sell (payroll system solutions) and instead focused on the outcome for the client (saving millions).

If what we're doing is not generating enough income to sustain our lifestyle, then it's called a hobby. We can feel great when we do it, but typically we would need another source of income. That's why it's really important to communicate the value of what we do. Authentic influence is about making a difference that we want to make. It's about utilising our personal currency to contribute and make the world a better place.

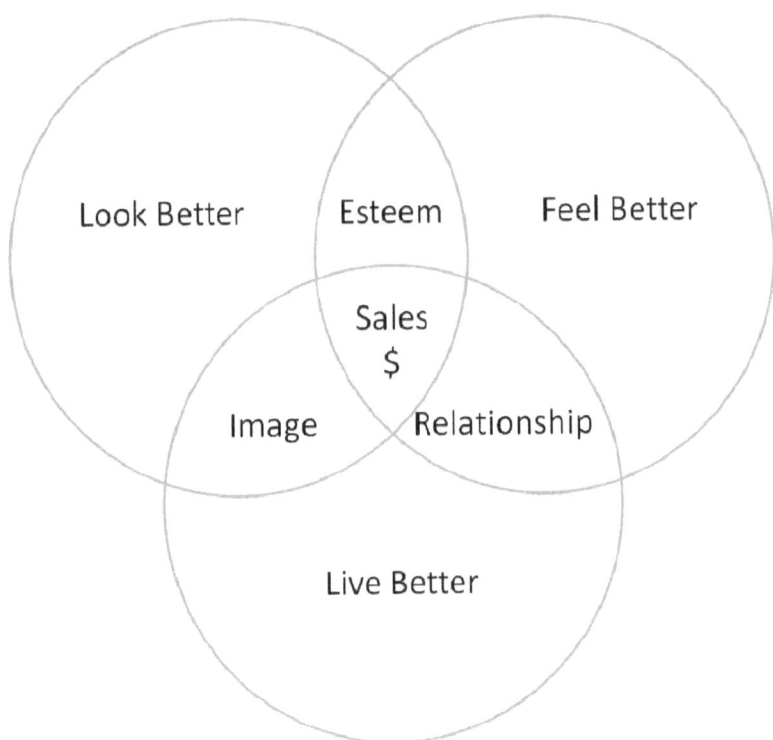

I believe there are fundamentally three types of consumer transactions that are driven by self-worth. We make purchases to:

- **look better to ourselves and others**
- **feel better about our relationship with ourselves and others**
- **live better according to our values and society values**

Looking better and living better relates to boosting our image, looking better and feeling better relates to boosting our esteem, and feeling better and living better relates to boosting our relationships and quality of life.

We all have unique values to contribute. Our value, based on our personal currency, comes from how we're unique and different. By structuring the contribution we make using a platform to suit our talents (e.g., working with people) and preferred mode of delivery (e.g., speaking), we position ourselves to being the best version of us.

We are a finite resource and valuing our time is part of honouring our personal currency. How does this play out in business? In a 2016 Catalyst Quick Take report, *Women's Earnings and Income*, the gender pay gap in Australia was reported to be at 17.3%, based on full-time average weekly earnings (based on WGEA gender pay gap statistics). Building on this in her book, *Women Don't Ask*, Linda Babcock, explains how men are four times more likely to ask for a raise than women and when women do pluck up the courage, they ask for *30% less*. This suggests women value themselves 30% less than their male colleagues. Yet, women have become the hottest commodity to organisations, due to our ability to build inclusive teams and cultures, and our long-range perspective which takes more into consideration than just the bottom line.

A Business Insider article titled, *7 Ways The Workplace Will Look Different in 2050*, explores how the workforce structure will be different by 2050. In this article, a University of Oxford report predicts that by 2030, we'll have lost almost 50% of the workforce to artificial intelligence. With this change to workforce structure, organisations will only employ a small number of people, and the majority of work carried out by organisations will be made up by an outsourced freelance project team. Think of Upwork (previously Elance). They're one of a growing number of online platforms dedicated to freelance workers. They allow you to seek out people with specific skill sets or post a job, and have freelancers bid for the projects they'd like to work on.

The first area of authentic influence is our relationship with money and how this comes across in our conversations related to money. Our non-verbal communication, specifically micro expressions, are a give away to our beliefs around money. If we believe we're charging more than what we're worth, then when we state the amount for our products, services or programs, our micro expressions will reflect this. Most people have a good BS detector and are good at picking up incongruent body language signals. We want to build trust and credibility and avoid incongruence.

Getting used to money conversations is especially important for women. I was once attending a training session where part of an exercise was addressing beliefs about money – not something I had ever considered up to that point. We all stood up and together we recited, 'My rate is … ' and each repetition increased our fictitious hourly rate by increments of $100. The purpose of the exercise was to notice what emotions and feelings came up internally as we continued to increase the amount.

What's your default amount? What's your daily rate? Annual rate? Project rate? I appreciate we recently discussed moving from a rate-based to a values-based business model, but go with me here! What amount do you subconsciously believe you are worth? Our 'rate' becomes an invisible earnings threshold. Beyond this threshold, we can't see, comprehend, or believe we could contribute enough value to receive that amount of money, so we don't!

Commonly, the way women set their fees is to search online or ask others, then based on what's being charged, price themselves just under the average rate. With this approach, you're not valuing your personal currency and it reinforces low self-worth. One way to overcome this approach is by shifting to a values-based model. Start with what value the product or service contributes and work backwards from there. Value might include:

- **time gained or saved**
- **improvements in retention, efficiency or productivity**
- **better health**
- **better relationships**
- **money gained or saved**

Here's an example: say you're a copywriter and you're great at what you do. It might not take you very long to put a press release together for a client. Despite completing the task quickly, the value it represents might be thousands of dollars worth of publicity (based on your track record of success in gaining media exposure for your clients). So the approach to pricing this is not based on the time it took you to write the press release, but the value of the press release to the client. If we continue to charge based on an hourly rate, we're stuck in a transactional mode. We need to move away from hourly rates, look at the value we contribute and modify the way we structure our pricing and our finances accordingly.

Authentic influence is about listening to our clients, customers and teams first. It's arrogant to think that we know the solution before we've explored what the perceived problem is. The presenting problem is rarely the problem. When we invite conversation around the presenting challenges, we build trust, open up channels of communication and provide an opportunity to explore solutions not previously considered. It also positions us as someone who is credible, because we're showing we care. Ultimately, we don't want to be working with a client when they're not a match for us. If we honestly feel there's a more suitable solution than what we offer, then refer them on graciously.

With clients I've worked with, particularly women in business, an area that seems to be overlooked or not set up properly is invoicing, and having a financial dashboard to track cash flow, expenses and performance targets. Statistically, the most effective pay-invoicing cycle is fourteen days or less. I've worked with clients who've had sixty-day invoicing cycles. For small businesses, this is a long time to be carrying costs. If you're a small business owner, check your invoicing cycle – how might a fourteen-day invoicing cycle work for you?

It's vital to measure your spending for one month, if you haven't already done so, to keep track of where it goes. There are some great simple online tools now that do this really well. MYOB and Xero are well-known programs and there are other excellent user-friendly alternatives available too. Another suggestion to value what you do and your time, is to structure different levels of access to you. By doing this, you're communicating that working with you individually is more valuable and will be priced at a premium.

I want you to imagine a giant pyramid divided into five layers. Now map out your business offerings at different price points. Start with a no-cost option at the bottom and increase the amount for each level as you move up, with the top tier representing your most premium offering – you. As an example with my own business, I have a giveaway on my website, *Speak With Confidence* guide, at the time of writing this book. At the next level up, people can purchase a copy of this book. Above that, my Woman of Worth Program, Face-2-Face Trainings, and the Results Roundtable Mentoring group. At the top of the pyramid, the opportunity to work with me privately. Keynote speaking and corporate program facilitation are also part of the business model.

What are you offering at each level in your business? The first layer (no cost) is typically adding value by *telling* people what they need to know. The next level up is about *showing* people how to do it, via a book, podcast, video or another medium. The next level up from that represents your mid-range offering, working with clients as a large group (e.g., a workshop), or an online program. Above that, second from the top, this is your upper front-end offering. Here, you might be delivering to a smaller group (such as a masterclass with some individual access to you), or other business activities, such as keynote speaking. Finally, at the very top of the pyramid is your premium offering, where you work individually with the client and do some of the work for them. For example, as a copywriter, you write the press release instead of coaching the client to write it, and providing feedback afterwards.

Depending on the nature of your business, there will be adjustments of the layers. Regardless, the pyramid is a great model to visually create separate levels of access to you. With a finite number of hours in the day, you only want a small number of top tier clients.

These clients are the most time consuming (and probably more rewarding too). In contrast, down the bottom of the pyramid, you are offering a valuable book or resource that doesn't require any of your time to deliver.

What if you're employed in an organisation? How does this apply to you? If you're doing what you believe is an unnecessary amount of non-essential work, it's time to take a stand. Bring your courage and have that potentially uncomfortable conversation with your employer. Make your case based on objective facts, rather than opinion. For example, 'I feel my talents are better utilised doing X rather than Y; can we make a time to review what the priorities are and what greater work flexibility might look like? I've put together some examples I'd like to share with you?', or, 'I can work on the Davidson account if I pause on the Green account (show you have thought this through). I'm thinking the Davidson account has priority, but I want to check you're okay with this decision'. If necessary, it's easier to ask for forgiveness than permission!

Tim Ferriss' book, *The 4-Hour Work Week*, explores the concepts around outsourcing tasks that you might normally do in your day-to-day role to offshore. The goal here is to free up time to improve work-life balance or do more creative, strategic or specialised work that only you can do. I'm not making a specific recommendation to do this, but if it interests you, I highly recommend reading this book.

*Financial independence is the ability to live from the income of your own personal resources.*

~ Jim Rohn

For this next activity, I recommend finding a communication buddy. Stand in front of each other, feet hip-width apart, and take turns saying, 'My rate is' and then say an amount. You could be talking about hourly, daily, monthly or an annual rate – whatever works for you. The listener is looking for any flinching micro expressions on the speaker's face. Flinching indicates that the person has reached the rate they truly believe they're worth subconsciously. Give it a go; it's a really powerful exercise.

If you haven't already, get a dashboard that shows you money coming in and money coming out of the business. There are really only four categories of money:

- *what you sold* (**money that's gone into your account**)
- *what you think you sold* (**money you've invoiced**)
- *what you've spent* (**money that's gone out of your account**)
- *what you think you spent* (**purchases with credit cards that you've not paid for yet**)

A mentor once said, 'If you're opening your wallet or purse and there's no money in there, psychologically you're reaffirming in your mind, "I have no money"'. Always have money in your wallet – ideally your daily rate – so every time you open your wallet you are reaffirming you have money. This will emphasise and show you how much you subconsciously believe you need to survive. This is also a tactic I've heard a number of successful people subscribe to.

## Chapter Ten Practice

To cultivate your money mindset, make the following a regular practice:

- **Get clear. Find a buddy and do the 'My rate is' exercise. When you notice a subtle flinch, that's your belief about their rate. Give it a go, it's fascinating.**
- **Get confident. What outcome do your products/services deliver? Write these down.**
- **Get leverage. Change your invoicing cycle to fourteen days or less to improve cash flow.**
- **Get perspective. What amount of money do you believe is the maximum amount you could ever possibly earn, being the best version of you? Write this down. How different is this to what you're earning now? What needs to change to achieve this?**

## Your Chapter Ten Commitments:

What is one thing from this chapter you are committing to taking action on now?

(space for writing)

# 11
# Action Traction

*Done is better than perfect.*

~ Sheryl Sandberg

Action traction is the difference between being a high achiever and a perfectionist. The distinction: a high achiever is driven by a love of learning and a sense of purpose to make a difference to the space they're in, while a perfectionist is driven by fear, and an ambition to be perfect so others will think they're good enough and worthy. Perfectionism is a control mechanism. If we can't control feeling worthy about ourselves, we control things and the environment around us. By controlling, I mean micromanage our environment. We will be calling the shots so we get to do what we want, when we want and how we want.

Everyone has their own version of perfectionism, and they all contribute to exhaustion. Maintaining and controlling your environment takes up headspace, energy and occurs when you lack trust in your ability to adapt to the current situation or to a perceived future situation. Perfectionism is a lack of trust in *you*.

By controlling your immediate environment, you're making sure there are no surprises. It also means you don't have to deal with anything unexpected or risk being caught out. It safeguards against being judged as 'not good enough'. Pushing through procrastination to create momentum to get moving, is about taking action. People buy *you* more than your product or service. They need to be seeing *you*. This is why visibility and self-expression of your unique talents are important.

In communicating who we are, how we think, our likes and dislikes, we're communicating our authentic personality and this is where we shine as an individual. We won't be liked by everyone and we need to be okay with that. We want to surround ourselves with people we connect with, can relate to and also who inspire us and champion us to grow. I believe having a diverse network is a strength. A network which includes a variety of people, is a more rewarding and richer source of opportunity to create human connections, stimulate innovative thinking and foster future collaborations.

People who are similar, tend to think the same way. Sharing our thinking is helpful, insightful and valuable to others, but won't be for everyone. When we risk sharing more of who we are, we invite others to do the same. This is a base to begin conversations around things that matter. In contrast, if we continue to be who we think others want us to be and behave accordingly, there's a risk of unfulfilling relationships and conversations based on things we don't really care about.

From my observations (generally speaking), women respond to fear by hesitating and questioning themselves, whereas men respond by taking action. Is this genetic, social conditioning or a combination of the two? Either way, fear is a normal emotion, which means developing a healthy friendship with fear is desirable, rather than wishing we could avoid it altogether. A healthy relationship with fear, means building self-awareness about why we're feeling this way and acknowledging the personal growth opportunity. Developing a healthy self-relationship, becoming our own best friend and loving who we are is essential to feeling enough. If we don't love who we are, I believe a part of us still questions our worth. Perhaps this may be true for you?

In the presence of fear, hesitating and not knowing why, can be frustrating. Putting off that next step, even when we want the outcome, is a pattern I've seen and continue to see with clients. We will find ways and create elaborate excuses to not do what we say is important to us.

One approach I found effective in helping me move beyond internal resistance towards a project or activity that I wanted to do, but kept putting off, was getting clear about how I use my time. I'm a big fan of using a diary and I've switched from using a paper-based diary to an electronic version. This allows me to set up reminders, schedule recurring appointments, block out times and my favourite: colour code my activities. I start by putting in the things that are essential and non-negotiable. Then I schedule the remaining time with a mixture of activities that move me towards the goal I want to accomplish. A goal could be a work related, hobby related or personal growth related.

To schedule your diary effectively, you need to be really clear about what matters to you *now*. I like to choose a growth project that's work related (such as my Woman of Worth Program) and a growth project that's personal (taking tango lessons). There will be some days and weeks when we have more time to allocate these projects, and others where there'll be less time. What's important is the consistency. Small, frequent steps build momentum, create a feeling of progress and lead to a result. It's easy to lose momentum when consistency is not there. When you're clear about what's important to you, and what's going to help you grow and evolve, you're acknowledging that you're worthy of growing, worthy of learning, worthy of evolving, and you're committed to making it happen!

Recognising what we do easily and effectively, and what tasks take us a disproportionate amount of time, is important when deciding, delegating and doing. Sometimes, it may be more valuable to pay someone else to do what takes you a long time to do. Initially, you may wonder why you should pay someone else to do what you can do yourself. When you value your time and you're aware of how you're most valuable, then it becomes a no brainer to pay someone else. An example of this is getting someone to do your housecleaning. This would allow you to free up time to do something creative or get out and about, doing what you love and the things that matter most. When we're singing our song, we're more valuable, more visible and we're removing one more obstacle preventing us from moving forward towards what we want to do.

Outsourcing is one way of creating systems to streamline processes. With systems in place, we reduce repetition, so we can do something once and then replicate or delegate for someone else to do. Sometimes it's a matter of saying no to requests because we can't be all things to all people all of the time.

Moving beyond procrastination means that whatever we decide to focus on, the first step is being clear on what this is and why we're doing it. It's one thing to say, 'I'm going to have piano lessons' and another thing following through. We need to take our intention to the next level, so being clear on why we want to have piano lessons and knowing what outcome we want to achieve by doing so. What is that desire, that dream, that unfulfilled wish, we bring into our lives by having piano lessons? What is it that's compelling us to start this project now?

Most goals and projects have different areas. I regularly see clients write goals like, 'Get ten new leads this week'. This is not specific enough to make it easy to do and with goals as broad as this, the goal isn't usually achieved, and typically gets rolled over to the following week and the week after that, each time reminding the client that they didn't succeed. Sometimes goals are written when there's a lack of clarity about what specifically needs to happen. To give ourselves the best chance of success, we need to break this down into more specific action steps.

Continuing with the piano lesson example, let's say you want to take up this project to fulfil a lifelong dream of being able to play a particular piece of music. All projects need to be broken down into different areas and have a meaningful outcome. Just putting piano lessons on your To Do list isn't specific enough; it needs to be broken down into smaller steps. For example:

- **Research piano teachers within a ten-kilometre radius**
- **Call five teachers to find out more information, availability, expectations, pricing, etc**

- Select two to meet in person and book appointments
- Attend appointments and get a feel for their character and teaching style
- Select preferred teacher and book first lesson

You can see how breaking down this goal into smaller specific tasks, makes this seem more manageable and easier to do.

To free up some headspace, create your To Do Wish List. Think of all the things that you would like to do and write them down on a piece of paper. Keep going until you have everything down on paper. Looking at what you have, sort these into the following categories:

- **Now**
- **within three months**
- **within six months**
- **within twelve months**
- someday

This gives you an idea of general priorities and where your passion projects (non-urgent but exciting ideas) might work best in your calendar. Next, get specific with prioritising, beginning with activities in your *Now* category. What's on your list? Since I've been doing this, I continue to be amazed by how quickly I achieve some of the things on my list.

*I don't waste time. I move. I finish things. I don't try to do things to the nth degree. I know what's important and what's not ... I've learned what really matters.*

~ Gail Kelly

The next step is to create goals around these. I find doing my weekly goals every Sunday night very helpful. The advantage of doing my goals the night before, is so that when I wake up Monday morning, I know exactly what I'm doing, what I need and have clear direction for my day and the rest of the week. Each night before going to bed, I'll review my diary for the next day and make any adjustments needed. This helps remind me about what's on during the remainder of the week.

Initially, I write down everything I would like to get done and what commitments I have. I select three non-negotiable goals and commit to getting them done no matter what. I schedule my non-negotiables and add my other commitments in. The rest of the week I schedule in the other nice-to-have-but-not-essential tasks.

I find this approach has made a big difference to freeing up my headspace. I also feel a lot clearer and more focussed during the day. The other thing I recommend is using a colour-coded diary. I like to use green for revenue-generating activities, blue for networking, pink for self-care, orange for admin, purple of friends and family-related activities, and yellow for travel. If you're more of a visual person, you'll love this. It's also a powerful way of being able to scan your diary to get a bird's eye view of how you use your time.

What proportion of time are you doing self-care activities, compared with networking each week? If you have no pink in your week (no self-care related activities) that's feedback on how you're prioritising your time, and provides you with an opportunity to review and tweak your diary activities to make sure there is some pink in there. If you use a paper-based diary, use different coloured pens or highlighters. Take it for a test drive and see how it works for you.

## Chapter Eleven Practice

To move beyond perfectionism, make the following a regular practice:

- **Get clear.** Create your Now and Later list.
- **Get confident.** Write down which areas in your life, you feel you need to be in control of. When you decide to be completely okay with who you are, write down what difference this makes.
- **Get leverage.** Break down your projects using the Project Planning Template. This is located at the back of the book, in the Resources section.
- **Get perspective.** Colour code your diary.

## Your Chapter Eleven Commitments:

What is one thing from this chapter you are committing to taking action on now?

(space for writing)

_____

_____

_____

_____

_____

_____

_____

_____

_____

_____

_____

# 12
# Rapid Results

*Taking initiative pays off. It's hard to visualise someone as a leader, if she is always waiting to be told what to do.*

~ Sheryl Sandberg

There are three types of results: results you deliver, results you deliver when you're accountable and non-results (which are still results!).

Accountability makes a huge difference to the speed at which we achieve results, the quality of results and the type of result. Having a network of peers and colleagues who hold you accountable and to a higher standard is really important. I don't mean a network of peers who are sympathetic and say, 'Look, it doesn't matter, you've got plenty of time', but a network of peers who will say, 'Hey, how's that project going? Where are you at? Need anyone to brainstorm with?'. These are the people who support you, and give you more drive to follow through and do the things you've committed to.

Excellence is commitment to completion – saying I will do this and then following through. In my experience, it's easy for people to make a commitment to take action, yet few seem to follow through. This is one way to stand out and shine, simply by following through and delivering in a way that's authentic to you.

If you have a playful side, or a quirky side, honour that, so when you do follow through on your commitments, people are not only pleased, they experience the outcome along with your personality. A simple example of this might be, you told someone that you would email them through some information. Follow through by sending the information and in the subject line put a playful or quirky comment. It's a subtle, and effective way to be memorable.

Surrounding ourselves and being accountable to peers achieves more than if we're only being accountable to ourselves. With an accountability group, we experience more momentum, better focus, and we're opening ourselves to different perspectives and new ways of thinking. That's the value of a diverse network.

Setting ourselves up for success requires a combination of shifting any mindset blocks and creating an external environment to support the changes we're making. Creating goals with accountability is another way to assist you move beyond procrastination and perfectionism. By showing up and following through with commitments, we build momentum, reinforce our belief in ourselves and build confidence. Accountability is about consistent action and achieving what matters to us.

There's a saying that we are the sum total of the five people we spend the most time with. Who do you spend most time around? What are their results like? Do they care about you enough to hold you to a higher standard?

Through a process of social osmosis, we tend to absorb and become influenced by the thinking and attitudes of the people around us. When we surround ourselves with high-calibre people, we are exposed to their thinking and perspectives, share their journey and learn about helpful tools and resources that we didn't know about before. That's why it's important to find a tribe, a group of people, or a network who hold you to a higher standard. These are peers who you also commit to, take an interest in and champion their growth. You are genuinely interested to find out about their progress each time you catch up. Progress doesn't have to be limited to career-based progress, it could be a holiday they're planning.

Developing a mantra may assist you in creating the sort of internal environment that supports you to achieve better results. A mantra is a saying you repeat to yourself. This can be done out aloud or quietly. You can do it at home, in the car, or wherever you like. Repeat your mantra in your mind when you go to bed of an evening and first thing in the morning. Whatever messages your mind is being exposed to, you're reinforcing neural pathways each time you hear it or say it and that's proactively creating a positive environment for personal growth.

I recommend developing and using a mantra around your worth. It might be, 'I am worthy, I am loved, I am loving and I love. I deliver ten times the value I charge of my services. I am powerful, I am prosperous'. There is no right or wrong – whatever feels right and whatever feels a little bit daring! Feel free to mix them up to create a powerful environment in your mind. Repeating a mantra is easy to do and easy not to do. The results come through the doing, not the intention. Achieving results that are meaningful for you and contributing to your prosperity at the same time is making you more valuable.

Think of a bullseye. When you aim for the centre of the bullseye, you have more chance of landing on the bullseye. The more actions you take, the more arrows headings towards the target. Does it matter if you don't hit the bullseye, or if you're one ring, or three rings out? Maybe, maybe not. Either way, you are much closer to the bullseye than if you had nowhere to aim. Without being accountable to someone, you may not land on the target board at all.

Financial goals are individual and personal. For some people, they have a specific target in mind, while other people prefer to have a metric that's not based on money. There's no judgement here. I believe having a financial target creates a bullseye to aim for. Ultimately, financial freedom creates choice.

When you have reliable streams of income, you're creating freedom of choice. In the world today, being an employee with one source of income, particularly if you have financial commitments such as a mortgage, car payments, or school fees, is having all your eggs in the one basket. I believe there's scope and opportunity for each of us to develop other forms and streams of income. Even for salaried employees.

Working with a mentor is helpful to women in business for commercialising and packaging intellectual property (IP). This is something I love assisting clients with. When a business is sold, the value of the business is based on its profit times its multiples. Multiples are the assets – commercialised and packaged IP assets.

These could be licenses or products. They are separate streams of revenue and separate sources of income and is something my clients seek to create and build more of.

Having separate streams of income is a pathway to prosperity. This is about backing yourself, because you are capable of making this happen. Working with someone who can guide you creates a source of momentum, brings additional energy and a fresh set of eyes and ears to provide an outside perspective when you can't see the wood for the trees. That's a valuable perspective to have.

I recommend, developing your mantra. Build your worth; know your worth before you leave home each morning. Repeat your mantra every night before you go to bed, every morning when you wake up, when you're in the shower, sitting at traffic lights and in those quiet moments. It only takes a few seconds. Start cultivating your own internal environment of growth.

Accountability starts with belief in ourselves and commitment to take action. A commitment to do what needs to be done.

*Back yourself.*

~ Gail Kelly

## Chapter Twelve Practice

To experience better results, make the following a regular practice:

- **Get clear.** Create a mantra specific to who you are becoming. Repeat it morning and night.
- **Get confident.** When you're unsure repeat this phrase, 'I've got this'. Believe it and repeat it.
- **Get leverage.** Follow through on commitments.
- **Get perspective.** Find a tribe of quality people.

## Your Chapter Twelve Commitments:

What is one thing from this chapter you are committing to taking action on now?

(space for writing)

_____

_____

_____

_____

_____

_____

# Afterword

Congratulations on making it this far!

My wish is for your personal and professional success. Do the activities and notice the shifts. I trust you enjoy feeling more self-confident and more prosperous.

I thought I was self-aware, until I invested in coach training. As my self-awareness shifted, so did my thinking, the responses to my messages, the number of opportunities and my results. Initially, I noticed the feedback and comments on my confidence and composure, followed by a trickle and then a steady stream of women seeking advice for their business-related challenges. That's why I've created the Woman of Worth Program (launching late 2016) and why I wrote this book.

You don't have to feel unfulfilled. What if you lived life from a place of self-confidence? How about living a life feeling connected with what matters, with more clout and more choice? Or a life sharing unique talents and personal currency? For some, this may seem unrealistic, but if you've embraced and played with the suggested activities at the end of each chapter, you'll know it's possible to create shifts in your thinking, language, results and life.

I have enjoyed sharing these distinctions with you, and if there's anything else you would like me to discuss in Confidence Zone, a weekly laser-focussed insight for kerryngamble.com subscribers, please send me an email so I can respond and help you out on your journey. If you haven't yet completed the exercises at the end of each chapter, go back to these and invest the time to do it now!

Feel free to connect with me on Facebook or LinkedIn. I value connecting with women who dare to shift from deciding to doing. You can email me at kerryn@kerryngamble.com

Go forth, inspire, be the best version of *you*.

# Acknowledgements

With love and thanks to my family for keeping me grounded. To the mentors who have inspired me to become the woman I'm becoming. Special acknowledgement to Sharon Pearson, for your wisdom and generosity; I am eternally grateful.

To the rock star clients, I have the privilege of working with; your journey of growth and evolution are making the world a better place.

Gratitude to Louise Karch, of Brandfluence, for sharing your talents and my great book title. To Zahrina Robertson, of Zahrina Photography; thank you for my fabulous branding photos.

# About the Author

Kerryn Gamble is the founder of the Woman of Worth Program, and an expert in confidence and self-leadership for women.

Kerryn solves confidence-related business challenges via program strategy development, program implementation and facilitation, Keynotes and delivery of Leadership Programs. Kerryn works with ambitious women to grow profitable businesses.

She presents keynotes and masterclasses focusing on building the infrastructure women need to transform self-worth into business worth: why we do what we do, how we get results and identify what makes us valuable – our personal currency.

To find out more about Kerryn Gamble, visit

www.kerryngamble.com

You can also email Kerryn at

kerryn@kerryngamble.com

Websites:

www.kerryngamble.com

www.corepotential.com.au

# Working With Kerryn

Kerryn Gamble is an insightful strategist and totally awesome business coach and mentor. Thank you for your words of wisdom, constructive feedback and keeping me accountable. You have given me clarity of purpose, confidence to inspire and focussed results in business. The work we have done in the past six months has positioned me so well to write about what I've achieved and where the business is going for an award nomination.

– **Ros Weadman, Director,** Melbourne PR & Marketing

At a time when I was looking to expand and grow in my business, I chose to work with Kerryn. She helped me discover parts of myself that I had no idea were blocking me to my success. Not only did I clear away blockages, I also became very clear as to what my purpose was in my business. I found myself to be more certain and grounded as to who I am, as well as where I wanted to grow and expand in my business. Kerryn is very professional and comfortable to work with, easy to trust, and gets to the core issue of any problem. It was a pleasure to work with you and I am so excited about my future!

– **Caroline Seipp, Owner,** Direct Connection

Kerryn is a thoughtful, passionate and inspiring personal coach. She has a no-holds barred approach and, for someone who usually has all the answers, this is great! I learned more about myself and honed in on what my platform is. A true professional, I highly recommend Kerryn as a coach, and I look forward to working with her again.

– *Yakira*

I can highly recommend Kerryn as an excellent personal coach. I've been a Senior Partner in a Global Management Consultancy Business for nearly twenty years, and worked with Kerryn to help shape my own direction. I learned a lot about myself, what's important and what drives me in the next stage of my life. Our discussions were enlightening, energising and valuable for providing a measure of progress.

– **Grant Stephenson, Former** Accenture **Partner**

Kerryn is an engaging and warm presenter and coach. What I loved most was enhancing my understanding of body language. What I found most useful was confidence building, particularly relating to presenting to groups. She sets the standard high in her ownership of the room.

– *Alison Licciardello, Principal Consultant,* Etiquette and Eve

Kerryn clearly knows her content and made it fun, encouraging participation and growth of all attendees. What I loved most was the interaction, reinforcement of my current practices, tweaks to others and giving structure to my presentation style. Anyone doing presentations would benefit from Own The Room masterclass.

– ***Dianna Jacobsen, Director,*** Shine At Business

Kerryn is an encouraging and quietly confident trainer. I learnt a lot that I will be able to put into practice. What I loved, although found challenging, was the video exercise!

– ***Kay Morton, Life Coach,*** Morton-Tolhurst

A wonderful interactive workshop, Kerryn is an engaging speaker, her presentation was top notch and the content was excellent. What I found most useful is improving non-verbal nuances and how to improve self-awareness and self-confidence.

– ***Kerry Smith, Business Owner,*** myTimeyourTime

# Confidence Magnifier Guide

*Confidence is not learned, it's applied.*

~ Kerryn Gamble

Your guide to speaking up, taking action and being remarkable.

Get to where you want to go sooner and achieve success on your terms.

Get your free 22-page guide by emailing kerryn@kerryngamble.com with subject line: 'Confidence Magnifier Guide'.

Go forth and inspire!

# Kerryn as a Speaker

Kerryn Gamble is a keynote speaker and workshop facilitator. Kerryn is sought after to speak on the following topics:

**Say It Like You Mean It: Building Your Brand of Confidence**

- The five biggest career crushing mistakes women make and what to do about them
- Building leadership presence
- Talk Your Walk: Strategies for more empowered language

## Secret Women's Business: Creating Success On Your Terms

- Inclusion and diversity are the new black
- Making the leap and creating success on your terms


## The Strong Women Paradox: Breaking Through Invisible Barriers

- Why sacrificing femininity doesn't equate to success anymore
- Women – the hot new commodity for business success
- Our self-worth is our social worth – being a woman of worth

For enquiries, to check availability or request Kerryn Gamble as a speaker, contact:

0488 179 500

www.kerryngamble.com

kerryn@kerryngamble.com

# Woman of Worth Program

Guiding you from Uncertain to Unstoppable!

The vision: a world where every woman communicates with conviction.

The mission: close the confidence and achievement gap for women.

This is a unique online program that's part inner-work, part skills-based and part accountability.

- Are you tired of working and feeling like you're going nowhere?
- Would you like to have branding and marketing messages that reflect who you are?
- Would you like to speak with confidence and clarity?
- Would you like to develop products for your business?
- Are you uncertain about the next steps to grow your business?
- Are you ready to take action now?

## Why should you join?

- Transform your self-confidence
- Gain motivation through peer accountability
- Experience a variety of program delivery formats, to satisfy all learning preferences
- Learn how to master your messaging
- Pitch like a pro
- Attain leadership presence and influence
- Increase product creation

## What does it include?

Over three months you will receive:

- Accountability program
- Live fortnightly online meetings with Kerryn
- Guest presenters
- Contribution to a selected charity to empower women
- How-to videos

- Fortnightly worksheets
- Access to the online forum
- Unlimited email support
- Access to online content
- And more …

## How do I qualify?

- You are a career woman in your own business or about to start in business
- You are 100% committed to personal growth
- You are committing to be 100% responsible for your results
- You are willing to follow through on the program strategies and tasks
- You're prepared to leave excuses behind

## What If I can't make some of the live calls?

As with any mastermind program, maximum value and experience come from participation. Calls will be recorded and made available to you, so you can listen afterwards at your convenience.

## What If I want individual mentoring?

- Individual two-hour strategy sessions are available for $750
- Ongoing individual mentoring is available at $3,000 per month, depending on availability

**How do I get access?**

The Woman of Worth Program will be launching late 2016. To be kept in the loop, receive launch updates and additional details, email kerryn@kerryngamble.com, with 'Woman of Worth' in the subject line.

Are you ready to get serious about being a woman of worth?

# Resources

## Values Elicitation Activity

The path to experiencing fulfilment and happiness is to live by our highest ideals or values. To do this, we need to know what these are – not knowing contributes to experiencing frustration, pain and despair.

Our true values are found at the extremes of what lights us up and, conversely, what really bugs us. The following questions will help you discover a sense of your most important values and what contributes to your fulfilment. Write your responses to each question.

*What's a one-time example when I felt in flow at work? What was I doing specifically?*

_____

_____

_____

_____

*What was contributing to this?*

*When has my life felt most joyful?*

*What was contributing to this?*

*Notice your strengths. What are they?(e.g. supporting others, connecting with people, creativity)*

_____

_____

_____

_____

_____

*What is the main emotional theme around my strengths?(e.g. challenge, compassion)*

_____

_____

_____

_____

_____

*What do I spend a lot of time talking about? (e.g. family, the best restaurants, new ideas etc)*

_____

_____

_____

_____

_____

*What are my hot buttons and what do I get fired up about?(e.g. being cut off in traffic)*

_____

_____

_____

_____

*Where we invest time and money, shows us what we value. Where do I consistently invest my time and money?(e.g. clothing for kids, weekends away)*

_____

_____

_____

_____

*Results show where your values exist. Where in life do I have great results?(e.g. relationships, health)*

_____

_____

_____

_____

*According to the results I'm getting today, what values am I living by?*

_____

_____

_____

_____

_____

*From these responses, what themes am I noticing?*

_____

_____

_____

_____

*From the above list, what are my top five personal values? (e.g. respect, empathy, family, challenge, fun, etc.)*

1. _____

2. _____

3. _____

4. _____

5. _____

What values do I have that seem different, unique or special to me?

_____

_____

_____

_____

_____

# PROJECT PLANNING TEMPLATE

| My Project Theme is: | | |
|---|---|---|
| **My 3 priority areas for this project are:** | | |
| Area 1 | Area 2 | Area 3 |
| | | |

My Ideal Project Outcome Is:

| Project Start Date: | | Project End Date: |
|---|---|---|
| **Area 1** | **Area 2** | **Area 3** |
| Purpose of priority area 1? | Purpose of priority area 2? | Purpose of priority area 3? |
| | | |
| Ideal outcome for this? | Ideal outcome for this? | Ideal outcome for this? |
| | | |
| **List Action Steps** | **List Action Steps** | **List Action Steps** |
| • Tick when complete | • Tick when complete | • Tick when complete |
| | | |
| | | |
| | | |
| | | |
| | | |
| | | |
| | | |
| | | |

The personal and/or professional impact of this project is:

# Resources

Australian Bureau of Statistics. (2015) *National Health Survey: First Results, 2014-15.* Canberra. Available at: http://www.abs.gov.au/ausstats/abs@.nsf/mf/4364.0.55.001

Australian Government. (2016) 'Gender pay gap statistics'. Workplace Gender Equality Agency Available at: https://www.wgea.gov.au/sites/default/files/Gender_Pay_Gap_Factsheet.pdf

Babcock, L. and Laschever, S. (2007) *Women Don't Ask: The High Cost of Avoiding Negation and Positive Strategies for Change.* New York: Bantam Books

Babcock, L. (2003) *Nice Girls Don't Ask.* Harvard Business Review. https://hbr.org/2003/10/nice-girls-dont-ask

Begley, S. (2007) *Train Your Mind, Change Your Brain: How a New Science. Reveals Our Extraordinary Potential to Transform Ourselves.* New York: Ballantine Books.

Brown, B. (2010) *The Gifts Of Imperfection: Let Go of Who You Think You're Supposed to Be and Embrace Who You Are.* Minnesota: Hazelden Publishing

Cherry, K. (2016) *The Big Five Personality Traits: 5 Major Factors of Personality*. verywell. Available at: https://www.verywell.com/the-big-five-personality-dimensions-2795422

Carter, N., Joy, L., Wagner, H. and Narayanan, S. (2007) *The Bottom Line: Corporate Performance and Women's Representation on Boards*. Catalyst. Available at: http://www.catalyst.org/system/files/The_Bottom_Line_Corporate_Performance_and_Womens_Representation_on_Boards.pdf

Catalyst. (2016) *Companies With More Women Board Directors Experience Higher Financial Performance, According to Latest Catalyst Bottom Line Report*. Available at: http://www.catalyst.org/media/companies-more-women-board-directors-experience-higher-financial-performance-according-latest

Catalyst. (2016) Catalyst Quick Take: *Women's Earnings and Income*. Available at: http://www.catalyst.org/knowledge/womens-earnings-and-income

Changing Minds. (2016) *Values Development*. Available at: http://changingminds.org/explanations/values/values_development

Cook, G. (2013). *Why We Are Wired To Connect.* Scientific America. Available at: http://www.scientificamerican.com/article/why-we-are-wired-to-connect/

Cooper, M. (2013) *For Women Leaders, Likability and Success Hardly Go Hand-in-Hand.* Harvard Business Review. Available at: https://hbr.org/2013/04/for-women-leaders-likability-a/

Cuddy, Amy. (2012) *Your Body Language Shapes Who You Are.* TED Talk. Available at: https://www.ted.com/speakers/amy_cuddy

Davidson, M., Burke, R. (2004). *Women in Management Worldwide.* Aldershot: Ashgate

Deloitte. (2015) *Global Human Capital Trends 2015: Leading in the new world of work.* Deloitte University Press. Available at: http://www2.deloitte.com/content/dam/Deloitte/at/Documents/human-capital/hc-trends-2015.pdf

Dictionary referencing. Available at: http://www.dictionary.com

Dowd-Higgins, C. (2012) *Don't Let Imposter Syndrome Sabotage Your Career.* Huffington Post. Available at: http://www.huffingtonpost.com/caroline-dowdhiggins/impostor-syndrome_b_1651762.html

Drummond, S. (2016) *MasterCard says Australian retail sales 'worrisome'*. Sydney Morning Herald, February 23, 2016. Available at:http://www.smh.com.au/business/banking-and-finance/mastercard-says-australian-retail-sales-worrisome-20160221-gmzysx.html

Ferriss, T. (2011) *The 4-hour Work Week: Escape the 9-5, Live Anywhere and Join the New Rich*. London: Vermillion.

Frey, C. and Osborne, A. (2013). *The Future of Employment: How Susceptible Are Jobs To Computerisation?* University of Oxford: United Kingdom. Available at: http://www.oxfordmartin.ox.ac.uk/downloads/academic/The_Future_of_Employment.pdf

Goldberg, L. (1990) *An alternative "description of personality": Big-Five factor structure*. Journal of Personality and Social Psychology, Vol 59(6), Dec 1990, 1216-1229. Available at: http://dx.doi.org/10.1037/0022- 3514.59.6.1216

Journal of Personality and Social Psychology, Vol 59(6), Dec 1990, 1216-1229. Available at: http://dx.doi.org/10.1037/0022-3514.59.6.1216

Goyal, M. et al. (2014) *Meditation Programs for Psychological Stress and Well-being: A Systematic Review and Meta-analysis.* Journal of the American Medical Association, Intern Med. 2014;174(3):357-368 Available at: http://www.mindfulmanagement.es/wp-content/uploads/2014/09/Meditation-for-psychological-stress-and-wellbeing-copie.pdf

Han, E. (2016) *Women driving three-quarters of all retail purchases, going crazy on clothing.* Sydney Morning Herald. Available at: http://www.smh.com.au/business/consumer-affairs/women-driving-threequarters-of-all-retail-purchases-going-crazy-on-clothing-20160427-gofxs1.html

Hau, L. Lee. Billington, C. (1995) *The Evolution of Supply-Chain-Management Models and Practice at Hewlett-Packard.* Interfaces 25, no.5, 42-63. Available at: http://e3associates.com/files/Article%20-%20The%20Evolution%20of%20Supply-Chain-Management%20Models%20and%20Practice%20at%20Hewlett-Packard.pdf

Hogshead, S. (2014) *How The World Sees You: Discover Your Highest Value Through the Science of Fascination.* New York: HarperCollins

Hogshead, S. (2016) *How To Fascinate®.* Available at: www.howtofascinate.com

Haughton, J. (2014). *Moya Greene tackles 'Negative' Perceptions of Female Ambition*. Charted Management Institute. Available at: http://www.managers.org.uk/insights/news/2014/october/moya-greene-tackles-negative-perceptions-of-female-ambition

Kay, K. (2014). *The Confidence Code: The Art and Science of Self-Assurance – What Women Should Know*. New York: Harper Business

Lamia, M. (2011). *The Complexity Of Fear: Are you experiencing anxiety, or is it fear?*. Psychology Today. Available at: https://www.psychologytoday.com/blog/intense-emotions-and-strong-feelings/201112/the-complexity-fear

McLeod, S. (2014). *Attitudes and Behavior*. Simply Psychology. Available at: http://www.simplypsychology.org/attitudes.html

Mohr, T. (2014) *Playing Big: A Practical Guide For Brilliant Women Like You*. London: Penguin Random House UK

O'Neill, O. and O'Reilly, C. (2011) *Reducing the backlash effect: Self-monitoring and women's promotions*. Stanford Business. Available at: https://www.gsb.stanford.edu/faculty-research/publications/reducing-backlash-effect-self-monitoring-womens-promotions

Plano, C. (2016) *Your RAS: what it is and how to activate it for goal setting success.* Flying Solo. Available at: http://www.flyingsolo.com.au/startup/setting-business-goals/why-goal-setting-is-good-for-you

Popova, M. (2014) *Fixed vs. Growth: The Two Basic Mindsets That Shape Our Lives.* Brainpickings. Available at: https://www.brainpickings.org/2014/01/29/carol-dweck-mindset/

Radicati, S. (2014): 'Email Statistics Report, 2014-2018'. Palo Alto: The Radicati Group Inc. Available at: http://www.radicati.com/wp/wp-content/uploads/2014/01/Email-Statistics-Report-2014-2018-Executive-Summary.pdf

Rath, T. (2007) *StrengthsFinder 2.0*, New York: Gallup Press

Sandberg, S. (2013) *Lean In: Women, Work and the Will to Lead.* United Kingdom: Random House

Small Business Development Corporation, (2015) 'Facts and Statistics'. Government of Western Australia Available at: https://www.smallbusiness.wa.gov.au/business-in-wa/what-is-a-small-business/small-business-statistics/

Seierstad, C., Huse, M. and Seres, S. (2015) *Lessons From Norway in getting women onto corporate boards.* The Conversation. Available at: http://theconversation.com/lessons-from-norway-in-getting-women-onto-corporate-boards-38338

Shipman, C. and Kay, K. (2009) *Womenomics: Work Less, Achieve More, Live Better.* New York: Harper Business

Short, J. (2010) *An Intelligent Life.* Sydney: Random House Books Australia

Staik, A. (2013) *Toxic Thinking Patterns – How Pseudo 'Feel-Goods' Put a Hold On Your Brain (1 of 2).* PsychCentral. Available at: http://blogs.psychcentral.com/relationships/2011/07/toxic-feel-good-thinking-patterns-why-theyre-addictive/

Stranger, M. (2016) *7 Ways the workplace will look different in 2050.* Business Insider Australia. Available at: http://www.businessinsider.com.au/ways-the-workplace-will-look-different-in-the-future-2016-1#/#the-corporate-ladder-could-become-the-corporate-lattice-1

Strength Test. Available at: www.strengthstest.com

Wiseman, R. (2014) *Night School: Wake Up to the Power of Sleep.* Australia: Pan Macmillan:

Zenger, J. and Folkman, J. (2013) *New Research Shows Success Doesn't Make Women Less Likable.* Harvard Business Review. Available at: https://hbr.org/2013/04/leaning-in-without-hesitation

www.ingramcontent.com/pod-product-compliance
Lightning Source LLC
Chambersburg PA
CBHW021126300426
44113CB00006B/308